OXFORD
UNIVERSITY PRESS

Great Clarendon Street, Oxford OX2 6DP

Oxford University Press is a department of the Universiy of Oxford.
It furthers the University's objective of excellence in research, scholarship,
and education by publishing worldwide in

Oxford New York

Auckland Cape Town Dar es Salaam Hong Kong Karachi
Kuala Lumpur Madrid Melbourne Mexico City Nairobi
New Delhi Shanghai Taipei Toronto

With offices in

Argentina Austria Brazil Chile Czech Republic France Greece
Guatemala Hungary Italy Japan Poland Portugal Singapore
South Korea Switzerland Thailand Turkey Ukraine Vietnam

Oxford is a registered trade mark of Oxford University Press
in the UK and in certain other countries

British Library Cataloguing in Publication Data

Data available

ISBN 13: 978-0-19-836117-6
ISBN 10: 0-19-836117-3

1 3 5 7 9 10 8 6 4 2

Printed in Italy by G. Canale & C. S.p.A.

Contents

Introduction   4

Autumn term

Unit 1   Place value   5
Unit 2   Multiplication and division (mental methods)   8
Unit 3   Multiplication and division (written methods)   11
Think about it 1: Stepping stones   14
Unit 4   Fractions, decimals and percentages   15
Unit 5   Fractions, decimals, percentages, ratio and proportion   18
Think about it 2: Secret message   21
Unit 6a   Handling data   22
Unit 6b   Using a calculator   25
Unit 7   Review 1   28
Unit 8   Shape and space: reasoning about shapes and measures   29
Think about it 3: Out of this world   32
Unit 9   Measures   33
Unit 10   Shape and space: position, movement and scales, solving problems   36
Think about it 4: Dot-to-dot   39
Unit 11   Addition and subtraction, problems and checking solutions   40
Unit 12   Number sequences   43
Unit 13   Review 2   46

Spring term

Unit 1   Place value   47
Unit 2   Multiplication and division 1   50
Unit 3   Multiplication and division 2   53
Think about it 5: Open sesame!   56
Unit 4   Problem solving   57
Unit 5a   Fractions, decimals and percentages   60
Think about it 6: Pinball wizard   63
Unit 5b   Rotations and reflections   64

Unit 6   Review 3   67
Unit 7   Addition and subtraction   68
Unit 8   Angles, 2D and 3D shapes, perimeter and area   71
Think about it 7: Racing around   74
Unit 9   Measures and problem solving   75
Unit 10   Ratio, proportion, data handling and problem solving   78
Think about it 8: Caged in   81
Unit 11   Properties of and reasoning about numbers   82
Unit 12   Review 4   85

Summer term

Unit 1   Decimals, fractions, percentages   86
Unit 2   Calculations   89
Unit 3   Shape and space   92
Think about it 9: Crossing the red line   95
Unit 4   Problem solving 1   96
Unit 5   Problem solving 2   99
Think about it 10: A Jolly day out   102
Unit 6   Division, decimals and problem solving   103
Unit 7   Perimeter, area, calculation and problem solving   106
Unit 8   Calculation, percentages, ratio and problem solving   109
Think about it 11: Winning ways   112
Unit 9   Calculation and problem solving   113
Unit 10   Fractions, proportion, ratio and problem solving   116
Think about it 12: Window shopping   119
Unit 11   Angles, graphs and problem solving   120
Unit 12   Review 5–Review 6   123
Think about it 13: Safety first   125
Think about it 14: Your rules   126

Glossary   127

Introduction

The **Mastermaths** series will help you have fun practising all the maths you need to learn. Read this page first to see how to use the book.

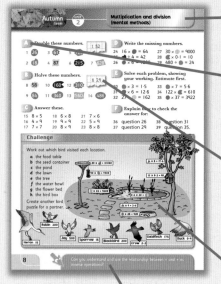

The title tells you what the page is about.

Work through the sections in order. Your teacher will tell you which questions to answer.

Some sections have examples to show how to set out your answer or remind you how to do the question. For sections with no example, you must choose your own method. Ask your teacher if you need help.

At the end of each page is a **Challenge**. Can you use the maths skills you have learned to solve the puzzles?

When you have finished working on a page, check that you can do this.

The **Think about it...** pages are fun games and activities for you to try.

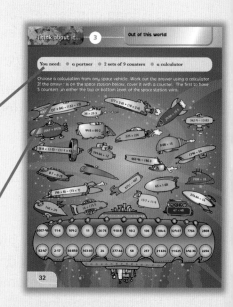

Check that you have everything you need before you start.

Read the instructions carefully to make sure you know what to do. Ask your teacher if you don't understand.

This book also contains six **Review** pages. Work through the questions in order to see if you have understood all the maths in the **Units**.

A Answer these.

1 64 × 10
2 465 × 10
3 132 × 10
4 5627 × 10
5 490 ÷ 10
6 3270 ÷ 10
7 6200 ÷ 100
8 6951 × 10
9 9500 ÷ 100
10 4965 × 10
11 5196 × 100

B Write in words.

12 3496
13 53 125
14 60 942
15 512 635
16 560 098
17 1 234 567
18 2 943 601
19 8 643 279

C Children in the same family are holding up cards with the same value. Name the children in each family.

20 Jack's family

20 Jack, Arthur, Fran

21 Max's family
22 Joe's family
23 Anna's family

Arthur 63000 ÷ 100

Sam 0·63 × 100 × 100

Anna 9000 ÷ 10 ÷ 10

Sarah 6·3 × 10 × 10 × 10

Ben 0·9 × 10 × 10

Carl 9000 ÷ 100

Sally 0·09 × 1000

Jack 6·3 × 10 × 10

Joe 0·9 × 1000

Max 630 × 10

Fran 6300 ÷ 10

Challenge

Play with a partner. Use two counters and a dice.

Each place a counter on the START section.

In turn, roll the dice and count round the track.

Find the green section that matches your dice number and calculate the answer.

For example, 3·8 × 10 × 10 = 380

The player with the higher number scores a point. First to 8 points wins the game.

START 33	8·3	3·8	830	0·38
0·33	×10×10	×10×100	×1000	3·3
0·83	×10	×100	×10×10×10	380
38	330	3800	83	8300

Can you multiply and divide decimals by 10 or 100 and integers by 1000?

5

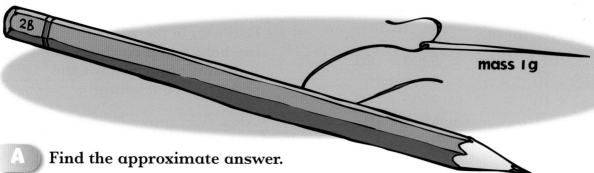

mass 1 g

A Find the approximate answer.

1 10 times the length of the pencil
2 1000 times longer than the pencil
3 $\frac{1}{10}$ of the length of the pencil
4 100 times the width of your little finger
5 1000 times the length of your table
6 $\frac{1}{100}$ of the width of this page
7 100 times the mass of the needle
8 1000 times the mass of the needle
9 10 000 times the mass of the needle
10 100 times smaller than the length of a metre rule

B Find how many times larger each number is.

11 4200 than 42
12 3800 than 38
13 4000 than 4
14 98 than 0·98
15 620 than 0·62   16 9000 than 0·9

| 11 100 times |

C Find how many times smaller each number is.

17 6·8 than 6800
18 29 than 29 000
19 36 than 3600
20 3·4 than 340

| 17 1000 times |

Challenge

Use a calculator. Only use these keys:

a	46	4600	f	3600	3·6
b	4·9	49	g	2·35	2350
c	68	68 000	h	47·20	47·2
d	0·37	370	i	34·8	0·348
e	3·6	0·36			

Write down the keys you think you will need to press to change each yellow number to the green number. Check your answers on a calculator.

Can you explain the effect of multiplying and dividing decimals by 10 or 100 and integers by 1000?

A Solve these problems.

1 John saves 20p coins in a bottle. When he empties the bottle he has 55 of them. How much has he collected?

2 10 sticks of rock cost £5·80. What is the cost of 1 stick?

3 In her till, a shopkeeper has £580 worth of £10 notes. How many £10 notes are in the till?

4 When the money is collected at the school fair there are 589 10p coins. What is the total value of the 10p coins?

5 A shopkeeper buys 1000 light bulbs each costing £1·50. What is the total cost of the bulbs?

6 5 cans of Fizzo cost £1·85. What is the cost of 33 cans of Fizzo?

7 100 people share the first prize of £643 200 in a lottery. One of them is Lottie Winner. If Lottie gives $\frac{1}{10}$ of her winnings to charity, how much does she keep?

8 2000 tickets are sold for a pop concert. If each ticket costs £5·35, how much money is collected from ticket sales?

9 A bus ride in Paris costs 1·68 euros. If I buy 10 tickets, how much change will I receive from a 50 euro note?

10 There are 10 sweets in a pack and 10 packs in a box. There are 10 boxes in a case and 10 cases in a crate. How many sweets are there in 2 crates?

11 A shopkeeper pays £432 for a crate of lemonade. Inside the crate there are 100 boxes and each box holds 10 bottles. If he sells each bottle for 72p, how much profit does he make?

Challenge

At each junction, work out the amount of money. Follow the correct path to find which bank Mia Money is visiting.

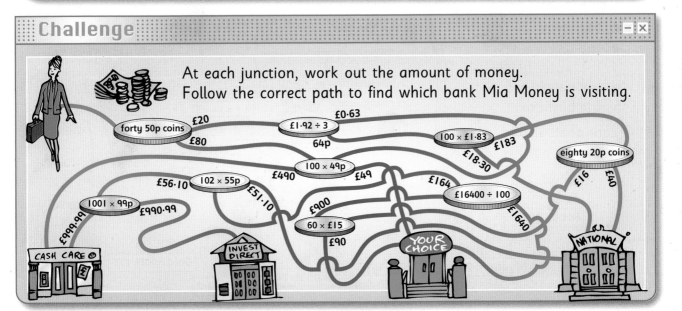

Can you solve word problems involving numbers and quantities based on 'real life' or money using one or more steps?

7

A Double these numbers.

 1 52

1 **26**   3 **61**   5 **120**

2 **18**   4 **87**   6 **215**   7 **628**

B Halve these numbers.

8 29

8 **58**   10 **160**   12 **310**

9 **84**   11 **340**   13 **560**   14 **486**

C Answer these.

15 8×5 18 6×8 21 7×6

16 4×9 19 9×9 22 5×9

17 7×7 20 8×9 23 8×8

D Write the missing numbers.

24 $16 \times \bullet = 64$ 27 $30 \times \bullet = 9000$

25 $\bullet \div 4 = 42$ 28 $\bullet \times 0{\cdot}1 = 10$

26 $\bullet \times 6 = 1200$ 29 $480 \div \bullet = 24$

E Solve each problem, showing your working. Estimate first.

30 $\bullet \times 3 = 1{\cdot}5$ 33 $\bullet \times 7 = 5{\cdot}6$

31 $\bullet \times 6 = 12{\cdot}6$ 34 $122 \times \bullet = 610$

32 $27 \times \bullet = 162$ 35 $\bullet \times 37 = 3922$

F Explain how to check the answer for:

36 question 26   38 question 31

37 question 29   39 question 35.

Challenge

Work out which bird visited each location.

 a the food table
 b the seed container
 c the pond
 d the lawn
 e the tree
 f the water bowl
 g the flower bed
 h the bird box

Create another bird puzzle for a partner.

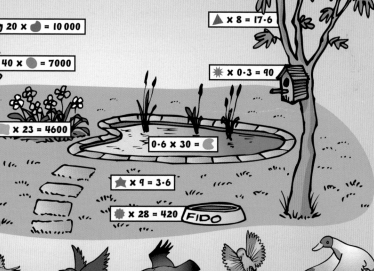

$20 \times \bullet = 10\,000$

$40 \times \bullet = 7000$

$\blacktriangle \times 8 = 17{\cdot}6$

$\ast \times 0{\cdot}3 = 90$

$\blacksquare \times 23 = 4600$

$0{\cdot}6 \times 30 = \bullet$

$\bigstar \times 9 = 3{\cdot}6$

$\bullet \times 28 = 420$ FIDO

Robin 300

Jay 500   Sparrow 18   Blackbird 200   Crow 2·2   Goldfinch 175   Duck 0·4

Heron 15

Can you understand and use the relationship between × and ÷ as inverse operations?

A Answer each question. Show your working.

1 45 × 22

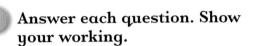
2 65 × 14

3 35 × 31

4 25 × 32

5 25 × 47

6 850 ÷ 25

7 1200 ÷ 25

B Answer each question. Show your working.

8 140 × 22	11 900 ÷ 25
9 250 × 13	12 10 000 ÷ 250
10 360 × 16	13 370 × 15

C Copy and complete this table up to 15 × 28.

1 × 28 = 28
2 × 28 =
3 × 28 =

D Use your table to answer these.

14 16 × 28	17 50 × 28
15 20 × 28	18 63 × 28
16 25 × 28	19 130 × 28

Challenge

Zen has emailed you from Argon. He does not know how to do some calculations. Write an email to Zen to explain how he can do his calculations. Here are Zen's problems.

46 × 25

1600 ÷ 25

62 × 13

59 × 8

380 × 50

6500 ÷ 250

19 × 28

Can you use related facts, including doubling and halving, to solve × and ÷ problems?

9

A Solve each problem, showing your working. Estimate first.

1 There are 45 apples in a box. How many apples in 19 boxes?

2 Seats for a concert cost £25. What will be the cost of seats for a group of 37 people?

3 A baker makes 720 buns and packs them in bags of 12. How many bags does he pack?

4 In a class of 28, each child needs 24 counters for a game. How many counters are needed?

5 For a school concert, chairs are put out in rows of 15. If 26 rows are set out and 345 people come to the concert, how many chairs will be empty?

6 480 jars of jam are packed in 16 boxes. If there is the same number of jars in each box, how many jars are there in 6 boxes?

7 3 bricks placed end-to-end stretch 64·5 cm. If the bricks are all the same length, how many bricks will be needed to stretch $21\frac{1}{2}$ metres?

8 A magician takes a 22 cm length of string and cuts off $\frac{1}{10}$ of it. He blows on the piece he has left and by magic it is suddenly 3 times its original length. How long is this new piece of string?

9 I think of a number, subtract 3·8, multiply by 25 and add 84·9. My answer is 1059·9. What was my number?

10 Write a prime number to fit each number statement.

$$35 < \bullet < 41$$
$$24 \le \bullet \le 29$$
$$67 > \bullet > 60$$

11 Multiply together the 3 prime numbers from question 10. What is your answer?

Challenge

Play with a partner. Use 2 sets of 12 counters. Take turns to choose 2 of the red numbers. Find the product of your 2 numbers. If the answer is on a rocket, cover it with a counter. The first with 4 counters on any rocket wins the game.

14   25   68   43   36   52   27   80   15

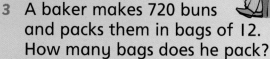

Rocket 1: 3536 1300 972 2160 405 602

Rocket 2: 1020 1836 675 210 780 1548

Rocket 3: 504 1120 645 952 1075 900

Can you solve problems about numbers in 'real life', choosing the appropriate operation?

A Use short multiplication to answer these.

1	327 × 4	4	519 × 6	7	567 × 3
2	231 × 5	5	483 × 8	8	894 × 7
3	423 × 7	6	962 × 9		

B Work out the exact answer for each. Approximate first.

9	32 × 19	12	36 × 18	15	74 × 22
10	43 × 17	13	37 × 45		
11	28 × 27	14	26 × 16		

C Use short division to answer these.

16	324 ÷ 3	18	434 ÷ 7	20	525 ÷ 8
17	765 ÷ 9	19	421 ÷ 6		

D Use the grid method to find each exact answer. Estimate first.

21

×	4	6	2	7
4	16 000	2400	80	28

16 000 + 2400 + 80 + 28 = 18 508

21	4627 × 4	28	54 × 38
22	3697 × 3	29	29 × 35
23	5176 × 5	30	425 × 24
24	4863 × 7	31	376 × 32
25	5862 × 8	32	495 × 28
26	46 × 38	33	625 × 47
27	37 × 26		

Challenge ⊟⊠

What two numbers have been multiplied together in each grid? Copy and complete each grid writing the missing numbers. Work out the answer to each multiplication.

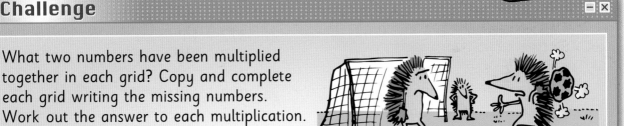

a

×	◖	★	⬟	⬢
⬢	32 000	400	120	20

b

×	⬢	▲	●	★
★	18 000	5400	420	24

c

×	▲	◼	✳
●	12 000	600	210
5	⬢	★	◼

d

×	✳	◖	◼
4	●	▲	⬢
⬟	6300	420	14

Can you approximate first and then use the grid method for ThHTU × U and HTU × TU?

11

A Use the grid method to find each exact answer. Estimate first and say whether your estimate is larger or smaller than the actual answer.

1 estimate 16, larger than actual answer

×	3	0·8	0·04
4	12	3·2	0·16

12 + 3·2 + 0·16 = 15·36

1	3·84 × 4	5	5·26 × 7	9	7·26 × 5
2	2·74 × 5	6	6·07 × 8	10	8·67 × 6
3	3·73 × 6	7	5·69 × 9	11	3·27 × 9
4	2·89 × 4	8	4·38 × 4		

B Find which 2 numbers have been multiplied together in each grid.

12

×	●	⬢	★
▲	18	0	0·27

13

×	◗	●	●
⬟	30	3·6	0·42

14

×	▧	✹	◆
✳	21	4·9	0·56

C Use a chunking method to answer these.

15	464 ÷ 16
16	390 ÷ 15
17	846 ÷ 18
18	552 ÷ 24
19	893 ÷ 19
20	988 ÷ 26
21	372 ÷ 14
22	587 ÷ 24
23	769 ÷ 18
24	967 ÷ 34

```
15    4 6 4
    - 3 2 0   (16 × 20)
      1 4 4
    -   8 0   (16 × 5)
        6 4
    -   6 4   (16 × 4)

    answer 29
```

Challenge

Dinah Sore wants to know how large this creature is. Help her to find out by answering each question on her cage. Add your answers together. Enter the total in a calculator. Turn the calculator upside down.

29 × 18
3654 × 6
167 × 23

24 × 26
792 ÷ 18
663 ÷ 13

7·14 × 4
4·27 × 6
2054 × 3
1493 × 8

Can you use a written method for multiplication of numbers with up to 2 decimal places?

A Solve each problem. Estimate first.

1 There are 8 blocks of seats in a stadium. In each block there are 2564 seats. How many seats are there altogether in the stadium?

2 A ferry can carry 2368 people. How many people can be carried in 8 trips?

3 A builder needs 650 nails. If nails are sold in packs of 36, how many packs must he buy?

4 Train carriages can carry 46 people. How many carriages will be needed for 985 people?

B Answer these. Use a calculator.

5 Parents at Colesby School have given £1200 for gym mats. If the mats cost £42·60 each, how many can the school buy?

6 It takes 2·27 m from a roll of fabric to make a tablecloth. How many tablecloths can be made from a roll of 46·5 m?

7 If one drawer holds 38 files, how many drawers will be needed for 726 files?

C Find the missing numbers.

8 $42·36 \times$ ★ $= 296·52$
9 $33·79 \times$ ● $= 270·32$
10 $26·78 \times$ ⬟ $= 160·68$
11 ✸ $\times 9 = 195·12$
12 ● $\times 7 = 207·41$
13 ◼ $\times 9 = 493·38$
14 $8·7 \times$ ◼ $\times 9·6 = 626·4$
15 $2·9 \times$ ⬤ $\times 8·5 = 73·95$
16 $87·9 + ($ ● $\times 3·8) = 116·02$
17 $12·8 \times (38·2 +$ ▲ $) = 739·84$

8 7

Challenge ─ □ ✕

Multiply each orange number by a number to one place of decimals to get as close as you can to the green target number. Use a calculator to check your answer. If you are within 50 of the target number score 1 point, within 25 score 2 points, within 10 score 5 points or within 5 score 10 points.
How many points can you score?
For example, 54·8 target 386, choose 7·2, $54·8 \times 7·2 = 394·56$, score 5 points.

54·8 target 386	62·4 target 362
39 target 427	18·7 target 230
26·2 target 237	33·8 target 693
14·7 target 125	26·7 target 283
11·9 target 380	83·3 target 483

Try again with 10 of your own numbers and targets.

You need: ● a partner   ● 2 sets of 12 coloured counters   ● a dice

Each place a counter on START.
Take turns to roll the dice and count around the stepping stones.
Answer the question you land on.
If the answer is on one of the hexagons, cover it with a counter.
The first to link their zones with counters over the hexagons is the winner.

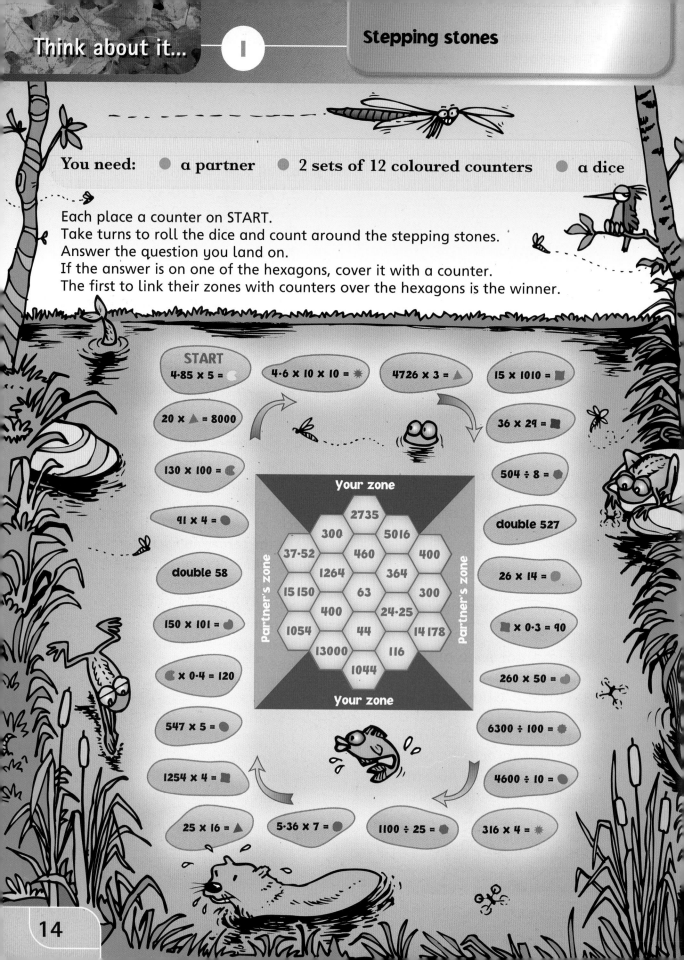

START
4·85 × 5 = ●

4·6 × 10 × 10 = ✳

4726 × 3 = ▲

15 × 1010 = ▮

20 × ▲ = 8000

36 × 29 = ▮

130 × 100 = ●

504 ÷ 8 = ⬠

91 × 4 = ●

double 527

double 58

26 × 14 = ●

150 × 101 = ●

▮ × 0·3 = 90

● × 0·4 = 120

260 × 50 = ●

547 × 5 = ●

6300 ÷ 100 = ✳

1254 × 4 = ▮

4600 ÷ 10 = ●

25 × 16 = ▲

5·36 × 7 = ●

1100 ÷ 25 = ●

316 × 4 = ✳

Your zone

Partner's zone

Partner's zone

2735

300   5016

37·52   460   400

1264   364

15 150   63   300

400   24·25

1054   44   14 178

13000   116

1044

Your zone

A **Write as decimals.**

1 0·2

1 $\frac{1}{5}$ 5 $\frac{1}{2}$ 9 $\frac{3}{5}$

2 $\frac{1}{10}$ 6 $\frac{7}{10}$ 10 $\frac{3}{4}$

3 $\frac{3}{10}$ 7 $\frac{23}{100}$ 11 $\frac{9}{10}$

4 $\frac{1}{4}$ 8 $\frac{37}{100}$ 12 $\frac{11}{100}$

B **Change to mixed numbers.**

13 $\frac{27}{10}$ 17 $\frac{37}{3}$

14 $\frac{17}{4}$ 18 $\frac{68}{10}$

15 $\frac{16}{5}$ 19 $\frac{29}{5}$

16 $\frac{28}{9}$ 20 $\frac{62}{7}$ 21 $\frac{80}{9}$

13 $2\frac{7}{10}$

C **Find the larger fraction.**

22 $\frac{1}{5}$ or $\frac{1}{4}$ 25 $\frac{5}{6}$ or $\frac{3}{4}$ 28 $\frac{1}{6}$ or $\frac{2}{9}$

23 $\frac{2}{3}$ or $\frac{3}{4}$ 26 $\frac{7}{10}$ or $\frac{3}{4}$ 29 $\frac{3}{10}$ or $\frac{1}{4}$

24 $\frac{3}{5}$ or $\frac{2}{3}$ 27 $\frac{3}{10}$ or $\frac{31}{100}$ 30 $\frac{5}{12}$ or $\frac{3}{8}$

D **Copy and complete.**

31 $\frac{\bullet}{10} = \frac{20}{100}$

32 $\frac{\triangle}{10} = \frac{40}{100}$ 35 $\frac{1}{10} = \frac{\bullet}{1000}$

33 $\frac{3}{10} = \frac{\bullet}{100}$ 36 $\frac{40}{100} = \frac{400}{\bullet}$

34 $\frac{2}{5} = \frac{\bullet}{100}$ 37 $\frac{3}{5} = \frac{\bullet}{1000}$

31 $\frac{2}{10} = \frac{20}{100}$

E **Find 4 equivalent fractions.**

38 $\frac{1}{5}$ 41 $\frac{3}{5}$

39 $\frac{1}{4}$ 42 $\frac{5}{6}$

40 $\frac{1}{8}$ 43 $\frac{3}{4}$ 44 $\frac{9}{10}$

38 $\frac{2}{10}$ $\frac{3}{15}$ $\frac{5}{25}$ $\frac{20}{100}$

F **Write a fraction that is equivalent to:**

45 $\frac{3}{5}$ with a denominator of 15

46 $\frac{2}{3}$ with a denominator of 24

47 $\frac{4}{5}$ with a numerator of 12

48 $\frac{7}{10}$ with a numerator of 35

Challenge ▭ ☒

Write a fraction to make each statement true.

$\frac{3}{4} > \blacksquare > \frac{1}{2}$ $\frac{19}{100} < \blacktriangle < \frac{3}{10}$ $\frac{1}{3} > \bigstar > \frac{1}{4}$

$\frac{2}{5} > \bullet > \frac{1}{10}$ $\frac{4}{5} > \bullet > \frac{61}{100}$ $\frac{3}{5} < \bullet < \frac{3}{4}$

$\frac{7}{10} > \bullet > \frac{63}{100}$ $\frac{5}{6} > \blacksquare > \frac{2}{3}$ $\frac{1}{2} < \bullet < \frac{53}{100}$

Can you change a fraction to an equivalent fraction by multiplying or dividing the numerator and denominator by the same number?

15

A Reduce to the simplest form.

1 $\frac{8}{10}$ 6 $\frac{20}{100}$

2 $\frac{4}{10}$ 7 $\frac{32}{40}$

1 $\frac{4}{5}$

3 $\frac{5}{20}$ 8 $\frac{15}{50}$ 11 $\frac{16}{40}$ 14 $\frac{32}{100}$

4 $\frac{6}{8}$ 9 $\frac{8}{24}$ 12 $\frac{25}{40}$ 15 $\frac{16}{200}$

5 $\frac{4}{6}$ 10 $\frac{9}{27}$ 13 $\frac{15}{45}$ 16 $\frac{88}{1000}$

B Write in order, smallest first.

17 $\frac{3}{10}$ $\frac{1}{4}$ $\frac{3}{5}$ $\frac{11}{20}$ 20 $\frac{200}{1000}$ $\frac{1}{4}$ $\frac{3}{10}$ $\frac{2}{5}$

18 $\frac{1}{4}$ $\frac{1}{5}$ $\frac{3}{20}$ $\frac{3}{10}$ 21 $\frac{600}{1000}$ $\frac{2}{5}$ $\frac{1}{2}$ $\frac{11}{20}$

19 $\frac{16}{20}$ $\frac{3}{4}$ $\frac{7}{10}$ $\frac{3}{5}$

22 $\frac{1}{10}$ 26 $\frac{1}{3}$

23 $\frac{1}{2}$ 27 $\frac{1}{6}$

22 b

24 $\frac{1}{5}$ 28 $\frac{60}{100}$ 30 $\frac{5}{6}$ 32 $\frac{4}{5}$

25 $\frac{3}{10}$ 29 $\frac{2}{3}$ 31 $\frac{9}{10}$ 33 $\frac{7}{10}$

C Find the arrow showing the correct position of each fraction.

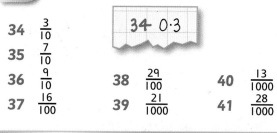

D Write as decimal fractions.

34 $\frac{3}{10}$

34 0·3

35 $\frac{7}{10}$

36 $\frac{9}{10}$ 38 $\frac{29}{100}$ 40 $\frac{13}{1000}$

37 $\frac{16}{100}$ 39 $\frac{21}{1000}$ 41 $\frac{28}{1000}$

E Write as fractions.

42 0·03   46 0·99

43 0·07   47 0·01

42 $\frac{3}{100}$

44 0·09   48 0·37

45 0·25   49 0·83

Challenge

Write in order the letters that show the correct position on the number line for each fraction or decimal fraction. What message has come through?

$\frac{1}{20}$ 0·5 $\frac{9}{10}$ $\frac{2}{8}$ $\frac{1}{5}$ 0·8   0·75 $\frac{1}{10}$ 0·1 $\frac{15}{20}$ $\frac{18}{20}$ 0·25 $\frac{2}{10}$ $\frac{4}{5}$ 0·3 $\frac{3}{20}$ $\frac{1}{2}$ $\frac{25}{100}$ $\frac{3}{20}$ $\frac{75}{100}$ $\frac{50}{100}$ 0·25

0·6 $\frac{2}{5}$ $\frac{500}{1000}$ $\frac{15}{20}$ $\frac{7}{10}$ $\frac{800}{1000}$ $\frac{19}{20}$ 0·4 $\frac{200}{1000}$ $\frac{4}{20}$ $\frac{400}{1000}$ $\frac{11}{20}$

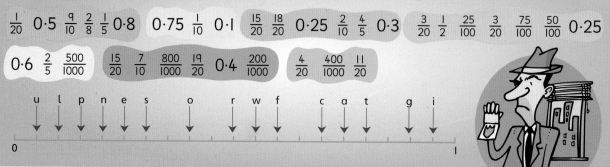

Can you reduce a fraction to its simplest form by cancelling common factors?

A Write in centimetres.

1 3·7 m
2 4·2 m
3 1·8 m
4 2·25 m
5 1·27 m
6 8·65 m

B Write in kilograms.

7 4300 g
8 2500 g
9 2200 g
10 2360 g
11 1472 g
12 8692 g

C Copy and complete.

13 $\frac{7}{10} = \frac{70}{100} = 70\%$

13 $\frac{7}{10} = \frac{\blacksquare}{100} = \bullet\%$

16 $\frac{2}{5} = \frac{\blacksquare}{100} = \bullet\%$

14 $\frac{4}{10} = \frac{\blacksquare}{100} = \blacktriangle\%$

17 $\frac{3}{20} = \frac{15}{\bullet} = \bigstar\%$

15 $\frac{\blacksquare}{10} = \frac{\bullet}{100} = 80\%$

18 $\frac{9}{10} = \frac{\ast}{100} = \blacktriangle\%$

D Find the answer.

19 25% of £500
20 20% of 3 metres
21 60% of 15 litres
22 15% of £220
23 75% of 840 kilometres
24 11% of £300

E Solve these problems.

25 If this line is drawn on the end of a line 1·362 m long, what is the total length of the new line in metres? _____

26 Which is the correct mass for a pencil: 300 g, 0·015 kg or 0·1 kg?

27 John has cycled 3·235 km. Kai has cycled 4·108 km. How many metres further has Kai cycled than John?

28 If 3·26 m of string are cut from a 5 m ball, how many millimetres are left?

29 There is 4·236 l of water in a 5 l container. How many millilitres of water are needed to fill the container?

30 It takes 35 g of a mixture to make a sweet. How many sweets can be made with 3·185 kg of mixture?

31 There are 340 children in a school. If 55% are girls, how many boys are there?

Challenge — ×

Use a set of 20 cards labelled 5%, 10%, 15%, 20%, 25%, 30%, 35%, 40%, 45%, 50%, 55%, 60%, 65%, 70%, 75%, 80%, 85%, 90%, 95%, 100%, and a set of 20 cards labelled $\frac{1}{20}, \frac{1}{10}, \frac{3}{20}, \frac{1}{5}, \frac{1}{4}, \frac{3}{10}, \frac{7}{20}, \frac{2}{5}, \frac{9}{20}, \frac{1}{2}, \frac{11}{20}, \frac{3}{5}, \frac{13}{20}, \frac{7}{10}, \frac{3}{4}, \frac{4}{5}, \frac{17}{20}, \frac{9}{10}, \frac{19}{20}$, 1.

$\frac{7}{20}$ 35%

Shuffle the cards and spread them face down across your table. Time how long it takes to arrange the cards in 20 pairs so that both cards in each pair have the same value. Can you beat your record?

Can you find simple percentages of whole number quantities without a calculator?

17

A Round to the nearest 10.

1 27   3 32   5 24
2 81   4 45   6 76

B Round to the nearest 100.

7 327   9 276   11 250
8 489   10 185   12 950

C Round to the nearest whole number.

13 4·6   18 9·5   23 6·52
14 5·8   19 1·72   24 4·91
15 2·4   20 3·45   25 6·03
16 7·1   21 6·28
17 6·5   22 8·37

D Find the complement to 100 for each number.

26 38   28 41   30 12
27 26   29 87   31 74

E Find the complement to 1 for each number.

32 0·2   34 0·35   36 0·29
33 0·75   35 0·63   37 0·43

F Find the complement to 1000 for each number.

38 600   40 150   42 650
39 250   41 850   43 950

G Find the complement to £20 for each amount.

44 £11·50   46 £9·85   48 £13·27
45 £12·20   47 £4·69   49 £8·89

H Round to the nearest $\frac{1}{10}$ of a metre.

50
◄–3·67 m–►

51
◄–5·29 m–►

52
◄–8·43 m–►

53
◄–14·75 m–►

Challenge

Follow the telephone lines by rounding each number to 1 decimal place.
Who is Crocko Dial talking to?

Make up a telephone puzzle for a partner.

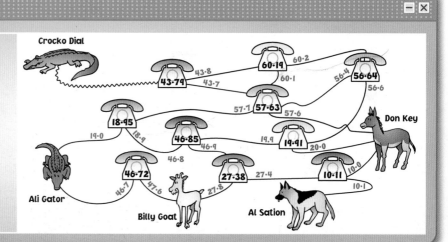

Can you round numbers with 2 decimal places to the nearest tenth?

A Find the decimal fraction equivalent to each fraction. Round to 2 decimal places. Use a calculator.

1 $\frac{1}{7}$ 8 $\frac{10}{17}$

1 0·14

2 $\frac{1}{8}$ 9 $\frac{6}{23}$

3 $\frac{1}{6}$ 10 $\frac{11}{50}$

4 $\frac{2}{7}$ 11 $\frac{5}{8}$

5 $\frac{4}{15}$ 12 $\frac{3}{14}$

6 $\frac{6}{11}$ 13 $\frac{11}{19}$

7 $\frac{5}{24}$

C In each set choose the decimal fraction equivalent to each fraction.

21 0·249

21 $\frac{249}{1000}$ 2·49 0·249 24·9

22 $\frac{23}{100}$ 0·023 0·23 2·03

23 $\frac{151}{1000}$ 0·511 1·51 0·0151 0·151

24 $\frac{16}{100}$ 0·016 1·6 0·16

B Find the decimal fraction equivalent to each fraction. Round to 2 decimal places. Write the fractions in order, smallest first.

14 $\frac{2}{7}$ $\frac{1}{3}$ $\frac{1}{8}$

14 0·29 0·33 0·13 $\frac{1}{8}$ $\frac{2}{7}$ $\frac{1}{3}$

15 $\frac{3}{8}$ $\frac{5}{16}$ $\frac{4}{13}$

16 $\frac{1}{12}$ $\frac{2}{21}$ $\frac{5}{23}$

17 $\frac{4}{5}$ $\frac{9}{11}$ $\frac{6}{13}$ 19 $\frac{6}{7}$ $\frac{9}{11}$ $\frac{15}{16}$

18 $\frac{49}{100}$ $\frac{3}{8}$ $\frac{5}{12}$ 20 $\frac{1}{11}$ $\frac{2}{21}$ $\frac{3}{19}$

D Write a decimal fraction to make each statement correct.

25 4·3 < < 4·35

25 4·32

26 2·95 < ⬢ < 3·1

27 5·98 > ⬡ > 5·97

28 2·69 > ◼ > 2·685

29 6·04 < ◖ < 6·05

30 4·314 < ◻ < 4·318

Challenge

a Find a fraction in the red box that does not have an equivalent decimal fraction (to 2 decimal places) in the yellow box.

b Find the largest fraction in the red box.

c Find the smallest decimal fraction in the yellow box.

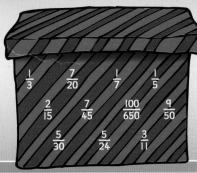

$\frac{1}{3}$ $\frac{7}{20}$ $\frac{1}{7}$ $\frac{1}{5}$

$\frac{2}{15}$ $\frac{7}{45}$ $\frac{100}{650}$ $\frac{9}{50}$

$\frac{5}{30}$ $\frac{5}{24}$ $\frac{3}{11}$

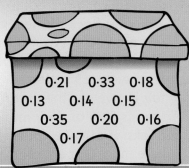

0·21   0·33   0·18

0·13   0·14   0·15

0·35   0·20   0·16

0·17

A **Find the ratio of yellow to green squares.**

> 1 2 yellow squares to every green square

a

b

c

d

1 in pattern a   2 in pattern b

3 in pattern c   4 in pattern d

B **Find the proportion of yellow squares.**

> 5 2 in every 3 are yellow

5 in pattern a   7 in pattern c
6 in pattern b   8 in pattern d

D **Using numbers to 3 decimal places estimate as accurately as you can what you need to multiply 18 by to reach each target number on a calculator.**

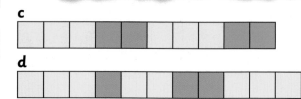

14 **100**   15 **95**   16 **700**   17 **334**

C **Solve these problems.**

9 In a sports club there are 4 girls to every 3 boys. If there are 42 children in the club, how many are boys?

10 On a school trip there are two adults to every group of 12 children. If there are 70 people on the trip, how many children are there?

11 In a class of 28 children 7 of them are in red house. What is the proportion of children in red house?

12 30% of a flock of sheep are black, the rest are white. What is the proportion of white sheep in the flock?

13 £1 in every £3 collected at a school fair is given to the library. The library spends 60% of their money on fiction books. If £1440 is collected at the fair, how much is spent on fiction books?

Challenge

Use a calculator. Choose a pink number from the pink box and a target number from the purple box. Estimate a number to 2 decimal places that you need to multiply your pink number by to reach your target number.
Write down the most accurate estimate you can make in 3 minutes.
Try again with an estimate to 3 decimal places.

17	19
37	
23	13

| 1000 |
| 100 | 245 |
| 79 | 1110 |

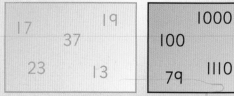

You need: ● cm-squared paper ● scissors

Copy the number grid onto cm-squared paper.
Work out the answers to the questions below.
Cut out the squares that contain the answers.
Place your cut-out grid over the word grid.
What message have you found?

Reduce these fractions to their simplest form.

1 $\frac{12}{40}$ 2 $\frac{9}{45}$ 3 $\frac{20}{150}$ 4 $\frac{64}{120}$

Find the smaller fraction.

5 $\frac{3}{5}$ or $\frac{7}{10}$ 6 $\frac{2}{3}$ or $\frac{7}{10}$ 7 $\frac{5}{8}$ or $\frac{3}{4}$ 8 $\frac{361}{1000}$ or $\frac{7}{20}$

Find the equivalent decimal fraction.

9 $\frac{1}{8}$ 10 $\frac{11}{20}$ 11 $\frac{45}{100}$

Find the complement to 1000.

12 625   13 810

0.45	$\frac{2}{5}$	0.85	0.1	0.4	375	$\frac{13}{15}$
0.375	$\frac{3}{20}$	$\frac{14}{15}$	0.95	$\frac{3}{8}$	$\frac{1}{5}$	290
$\frac{1}{4}$	$\frac{1}{3}$	0.5	$\frac{3}{5}$	90	$\frac{1}{15}$	0.15
$\frac{5}{8}$	$\frac{2}{15}$	275	0.125	$\frac{4}{15}$	$\frac{2}{3}$	$\frac{4}{5}$
$\frac{7}{10}$	$\frac{7}{15}$	$\frac{1}{2}$	0.9	0.65	0.55	0.75
0.7	190	390	0.625	110	$\frac{1}{10}$	$\frac{3}{10}$
0.875	0.25	$\frac{8}{15}$	$\frac{3}{4}$	$\frac{9}{10}$	$\frac{11}{15}$	$\frac{7}{20}$

The   leaves   on the   ground   were crispy.   Hardly

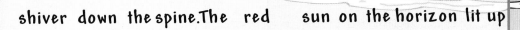

any frost   remained   but the   north wind   sent   a

shiver   down   the spine. The   red   sun on the horizon lit up

the c o u n t r y s i d e. The   island lying   about two miles

off-shore was hardly   visible.   One or two   leaves spiralled

through   the air   as the   wind   seemed to enjoy the sport.

John could not stop himself   from   running   quickly.

A Choose from these probability words to explain the chance of each event happening.

1 If I roll a dice I will score a 6.
2 If I spin a coin it will land as a tail.
3 In an hour's time it will be exactly 6 o'clock.
4 Tomorrow will be Saturday.
5 If I roll a dice I will score an even number.
6 I will eat before the end of the day.

1 poor chance

impossible
poor chance
even chance
good chance
certain

B Find the colour bags:

7 with a fifty-fifty chance of the first counter you pull out being red
8 with an equal chance of the first counter you pull out being red or black.

C Find each probability:

9 $\frac{1}{6}$

9 rolling a 2 on a 1 to 6 dice
10 finding a spade at the top of a pack of cards after they are shuffled
11 rolling an odd number on a 1 to 6 dice
12 spinning a number greater than 6 on a 1 to 10 spinner.

Challenge ▢✕

These are the scores of 2 players in a darts match.

Dead-Eye Dan

| 17 | 87 | 93 | 140 | 27 | 93 | 84 | 64 | 27 | 17 |
| 22 | 60 | 56 | 32 | 161 | 40 | 121 | 93 | 82 | 84 |

Hot Shot Hatty

| 53 | 63 | 81 | 27 | 135 | 29 | 101 | 140 | 36 | 48 |
| 70 | 51 | 16 | 89 | 64 | 53 | 100 | 15 | 67 | 102 |

a Copy and complete this bar chart to show the information.
b Write five questions about the bar chart for a partner.

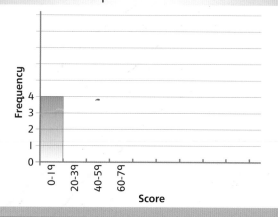

Can you present and interpret data on a bar chart with grouped discrete data?

A This pie chart shows how 24 children travel to school. Find the fraction of children:

1 who walk to school
2 who cycle to school
3 who travel by car
4 who travel by bus.

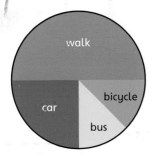

B Find the number of children:

5 who travel by car
6 who cycle
7 who travel by bus
8 who walk.

C This pie chart shows the colours of 36 cars in a garage. Find the number of cars in each colour.

9 18

9 red
10 blue
11 black
12 yellow

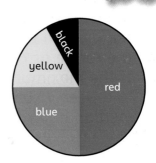

D Give the range, mode, mean and median for each set of prices.

13 £15, £23, £26, £23, £30, £33, £46

14 £48, £42, £54, £48, £48, £42, £68

15 £199, £203, £187, £199, £207

16 £0·64, £6·53, £3·68, £4·05, £0·64, £3·66

Challenge

Play with a partner. Use 5 dice and 2 sets of 16 counters.
Take turns to roll the 5 dice. If your scores have the range, median, mean or mode shown on the grid, cover the section with a counter. Only 1 counter can be placed at each turn.
The first to have a straight line of 3 counters wins the game.

Range	Median	Mean	Mode
5	5	less than 2	2
4	4	greater than 4	3
3	3	less than 3	4
2	2	greater than 5	5

Can you find the mode and range and begin to find the mean and median of a set of data?

23

A

Use the bar chart to answer these. Find each temperature for the first seven days in March.

1 the mode temperature
2 the mean temperature
3 the median temperature
4 the range of the temperatures
5 If the maximum temperature on 3rd March had been 7° less, what would the mean, median and range have been?

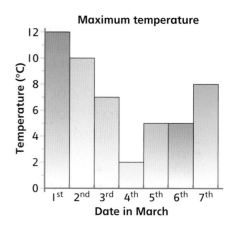

Maximum temperature

Temperature (°C) / Date in March

B

Use the conversion graph to answer these. Find the approximate number of kilometres.

6 10 miles
7 25 miles
8 45 miles
9 40 miles
10 30 miles
11 $12\frac{1}{2}$ miles

Find the approximate number of miles.

12 80 km
13 50 km
14 20 km
15 45 km
16 65 km
17 30 km

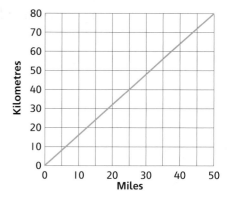

Kilometres / Miles

C

Using the darts match scores for Dead-Eye Dan and Hot Shot Hatty on page 22, work out:

18 the mean score for Dan
19 the median score for Hatty
20 the mode score for Dan
21 the mean score for Hatty
22 the range of scores for Dan
23 the median score for Dan

Challenge ▯ ✕

Play with a partner. Use 30 counters, a stop-watch and a sheet of cm-squared paper. Draw a coloured dot in 30 different squares on your sheet of paper. Ask your partner to time how long it takes you to cover every dot with a counter.
Record your time to the nearest second. Repeat 4 more times.
Now time your partner for 5 turns. Work out the mean time for the 10 turns.

Can you begin to draw and interpret a line graph, in which the intermediate values have meaning?

A Use an inverse operation to check each answer. Correct any answers that are wrong. Use a calculator.

1 wrong – correct answer is 4448

1 6317 − 1869 = 4438
2 4716 − 2349 = 2367
3 2509 + 6287 = 8877
4 465 × 23 = 14 880
5 743·88 ÷ 12 = 61·99

6 63·24 × 18·5 = 11 699·4
7 395·59 ÷ 13 = 30·40
8 3809 − 115·9 = 3689·5
9 437·6 + 18·09 = 455·69

B Copy and complete this table. Check each answer by using the inverse operation. Show your working. Estimate first.

	Question	Estimate	Answer	Check (inverse operation)
	623 × 14	8000	8722	8722 ÷ 14 = 623
10	365 × 98·4			
11	463 × 152			
12	8811 ÷ 33			
13	42 × 1·67			
14	9021 − 6892			
15	427 + 1698 + 248			
16	0·95 × 6			
17	261·8 − 7·35			
18	491·38 − 196·7			

Challenge   ▭ ☒

Shirley Knot has found her homework difficult. Five of her answers are wrong. Help Shirley by finding the wrong answers and working out how she has made each mistake.

a 13·4 − 6·8 = 7·4   **d** 47·36 + 28·9 = 76·26   **g** ⁻14 + 39 = 25
b 42 × 1·5 = 63   **e** 126·9 + 34·68 = 160·67   **h** 12·8 × 11·5 = 147·2
c 1008 × 12 = 84   **f** ⁻26 + 47 = 73

A Rewrite each calculation. Add brackets to make the calculation correct.

> 1 14 + (7 × 4) = 42

1 14 + 7 × 4 = 42
2 16 × 7 + 3 = 160
3 12 × 9 − 3 = 105
4 9 + 6 × 4 = 60
5 14 − 6 × 2 = 2
6 16 + 24 × 2 = 64
7 11 × 5 + 6 = 121

B Write two 3-digit numbers to make each calculation correct.

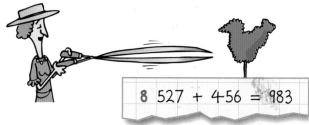

> 8 527 + 456 = 983

8 🔵 + 🔲 = 983
9 🌙 + ⬤ = 725
10 ⬤ + ◯ = 401
11 △ + ✿ = 830

12 ⬤ − ✸ = 179
13 ✳ − ★ = 264
14 ⬤ − ▪ = 123

C Write two 2-digit numbers to make each correct.

> 15 20 × 30 = 600

15 ★ × ▪ = 600
16 ⬤ × △ = 800
17 🌙 × ◯ = 1000
18 ✳ × ▪ = 250

19 ▪ × ✿ = 525
20 🌙 ÷ ⬤ = 900
21 675 ÷ ★ = △

D Answer these. Use the M+, M−, MR and MC buttons on your calculator.

22 (14 + 17) × (26 + 41)
23 (16 + 9) × (17 + 12)
24 (74 − 47) × (26 + 8)
25 (86 − 58) × (15 + 26)
26 (38 + 26) ÷ (91 − 75)
27 (108 ÷ 9) × (45 + 82)
28 (12 × 13) − (1242 ÷ 54)
29 (91 − 38) × (468 ÷ 58·5)
30 (9·8 × 12·5) + (6·4 × 14·5)

MC M+ M− MR

E Find which operation signs are missing.

31 (25 ★ 11) 🌙 (100 ÷ 25) = 9
32 (324 ▪ 225) − (6 ✿ 11) = 33
33 (14 ✳ 9) + (500 ⬤ 2) = 1126
34 (24 ✿ 4) △ (18 × 4) = 24
35 (25 🌙 24) ÷ (21 ★ 3) = 7
36 (247 ✿ 13) + (156 ✿ 89) = 264

Challenge ─ ☒

Play with a partner. Use 2 calculators.

> (⬤ + ★) × (△ + ✿) = 1470

You both have 5 minutes to find four 2-digit numbers to make this calculation correct. The person who finds a correct answer first or is the nearer after 5 minutes wins. Try another game with this calculation.

> (▪ − △) × (⬤ − ✳) = 672

Can you carry out calculations on a calculator with more than one operation using brackets and the memory?

A Find two consecutive numbers to give each product. Use a calculator.

1 156
2 600
3 812
4 1482
5 3192

6 2352
7 380
8 9312
9 10 302

B Copy and complete this table.

Numbers		Product
31	32	992
32	33	
33	34	
34	35	
35	36	
36	37	
37	38	
38	39	
39	40	

10
11
12
13
14
15
16
17
18

C Answer these.

19 $(32 \times 33) - (31 \times 32)$
20 $(33 \times 34) - (32 \times 33)$
21 $(34 \times 35) - (33 \times 34)$
22 $(35 \times 36) - (34 \times 35)$
23 $(36 \times 37) - (35 \times 36)$
24 $(37 \times 38) - (36 \times 37)$

D Answer these without using a calculator.

25 $(40 \times 41) - (39 \times 40)$
26 $(41 \times 42) - (40 \times 41)$
27 $(42 \times 43) - (41 \times 42)$
28 $(50 \times 51) - (49 \times 50)$
29 $(71 \times 72) - (70 \times 71)$
30 $(68 \times 69) - (67 \times 68)$
31 $(105 \times 106) - (104 \times 105)$
32 $(222 \times 223) - (221 \times 222)$
33 $(999 \times 1000) - (998 \times 999)$

Challenge

a Find which number you can enter into your calculator 8 times so that when you divide by 9 you find 8 consecutive numbers on the display.

Find 3 consecutive numbers that when multiplied together give the answer:

b 1716   **c** 15 600   **d** 29 760.

e Work out the rules for this puzzle.

- Start with 465
- $4 \times 2 = 8$
- $8 + 1 = 9$
- $9 \times 5 = 45$
- $45 + 6 = 51$

- $51 \times 2 = 102$
- $102 + 1 = 103$
- $103 \times 5 = 515$
- $515 + 5 = 520$
- $520 - 55 = 465$

Does it work for other 3-digit numbers?

A Answer these.

1 8000 ÷ 100
2 6800 ÷ 10
3 0·72 × 10 × 10
4 3·9 × 100
5 6000 ÷ 10 ÷ 10
6 0·6 × 1000
7 0·07 × 1000
8 28 000 ÷ 100

B Answer these. Show your working.

9 46 × 23
10 25 × 41
11 36 × 32
12 950 ÷ 25
13 24 × 28
14 102 × 28
15 4237 × 5
16 3682 × 7
17 1279 × 6
18 8309 × 8
19 2764 × 6
20 1837 × 9

21 2·36 × 5
22 5·83 × 7
23 3·94 × 8
24 1·76 × 9
25 7·35 × 7
26 3·96 × 4
27 720 ÷ 15
28 504 ÷ 14
29 986 ÷ 17
30 828 ÷ 18
31 984 ÷ 24
32 896 ÷ 32

C Reduce to their simplest form.

33 $\frac{8}{10}$
34 $\frac{64}{100}$
35 $\frac{25}{80}$
36 $\frac{12}{18}$
37 $\frac{80}{200}$
38 $\frac{120}{1000}$
39 $\frac{9}{81}$

40 $\frac{25}{625}$
41 $\frac{50}{1000}$

D Write in metres.

42 430 mm
43 382 mm
44 509 mm

45 636 mm
46 281 mm
47 999 mm

E Find the complement to 500.

48 150
49 470

50 275
51 360

52 85
53 396

F Find the decimal equivalent to each fraction. Use a calculator.

54 $\frac{9}{10}$
55 $\frac{3}{10}$
56 $\frac{18}{100}$
57 $\frac{37}{100}$
58 $\frac{141}{1000}$

G Work out the range, mode, median and mean for each set of test scores.

59 43 38 26 39 38 29 46

60 86 85 99 76 87 85 91

H Answer these. Use a calculator.

61 (16 + 19) × (32 + 17)
62 (49 + 17) × (79 − 48)
63 (81 − 29) × (15 + 36)
64 (42 × 16) × (972 ÷ 36)
65 (241 − 53) ÷ (1001 − 997)

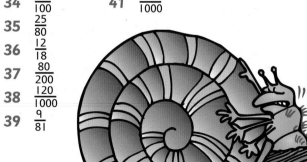

A On squared paper draw a quadrilateral:

1 with 4 lines of symmetry
2 with only 2 right angles
3 that has 4 equal sides but is not a square
4 with opposite sides parallel and 4 right angles but is not a square
5 in which the diagonals bisect each other but is not a square
6 in which the diagonals cross at right angles.

B Copy and complete the table for these quadrilaterals. Give two shapes that each quadrilateral could be and two shapes it could not be.

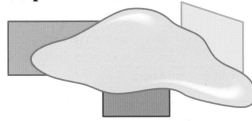

Quadrilateral		
Colour	Could be	Could not be
Red	Rectangle	12
	7	13
Yellow	8	14
	9	15
Blue	10	16
	11	17

Explain how you worked out your answer for each bright yellow section in the table.

C Draw these shapes on squared paper.

18 parallelogram
19 irregular quadrilateral
20 trapezium
21 kite
22 quadrilateral with one line of symmetry

D Write two properties of each shape.

23 rhombus
24 trapezium
25 kite
26 parallelogram

Challenge ▬ ☒

Use 2 dice and 2 sets of counters. Take turns to roll both dice. Find your total score from the list below. Cover one shape on the grid with a property to match. The first to have 3 counters in a line wins.

square	rhombus	kite
parallelogram	rectangle	square
kite	trapezium	rhombus

2 opposite sides equal
3 4 equal sides
4 only one pair of opposite sides parallel
5 all sides equal
6 4 right angles
7 both pairs of opposite sides parallel
8 adjacent sides equal
9 only one line of symmetry
10 no right angles
11 only 2 lines of symmetry
12 opposite angles equal

A Copy this Carroll diagram. Write the name of one quadrilateral that belongs to each section of the diagram.

1

	has 4 right angles	does not have 4 right angles
has 4 equal sides		
does not have 4 equal sides		

B Name a quadrilateral with these properties.

2 two pairs of adjacent sides equal and one line of symmetry

3 two pairs of parallel sides and no right angles

4 no right angles, one pair of parallel sides and one pair of opposite sides equal

C To the nearest half centimetre, find each perimeter.

5 the kite
6 the isosceles trapezium
7 the parallelogram

8 the trapezium that is not an isosceles trapezium

Challenge

Work out the perimeter of each garden.

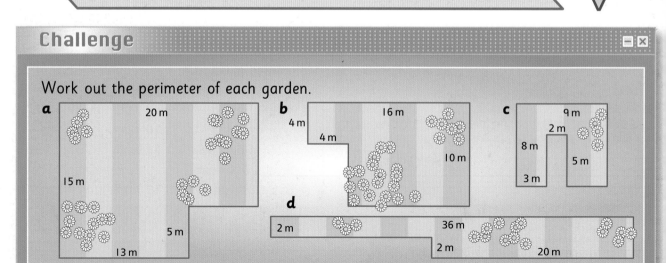

a 20 m, 4 m, 15 m, 5 m, 13 m

b 16 m, 4 m, 4 m, 10 m

c 9 m, 2 m, 8 m, 5 m, 3 m

d 2 m, 36 m, 2 m, 20 m

Can you calculate the perimeter of simple compound shapes that can be split into rectangles?

A — Find the area of each shape.

1						
		A				
				2		
					B	
3						
	C				**4**	
					D	
5				**6**		
		E			**F**	

B — Find the perimeter of each shape.

7 shape A   9 shape C   11 shape E
8 shape B   10 shape D   12 shape F

C — Use cm-squared paper.

13 Draw 5 different shapes each with an area of 9 cm^2.
14 Give the perimeter of each shape.

D — For a shape with an area of 9 cm^2, what is:

15 the longest perimeter you can find?
16 the shortest perimeter you can find?

E — Solve these problems.

17 Ivor Spade wants a garden with the three areas below. He wants to enclose them with the shortest length of fencing possible. Find the shortest length you can to help Ivor.

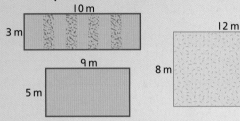

The path around this lawn is 2 m wide. Find the perimeter of these:

18 the lawn
19 the outside of the path

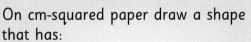

20 If grass seed costs 60p per square metre and paving slabs for the path cost £2 per square metre, find the total cost of seed and slabs for the garden.

Challenge

On cm-squared paper draw a shape that has:

a an area of 7 cm^2 and a perimeter of 16 cm
b an area of 8 cm^2 and a perimeter of 16 cm
c an area of 16 cm^2 and a perimeter of 16 cm.

Can you find the perimeters of simple compound shapes that can be split into rectangles?

You need: ● a partner ● 2 sets of 9 counters ● a calculator

Choose a calculation from any space vehicle. Work out the answer using a calculator. If the answer is on the space station below, cover it with a counter. The first to have 5 counters on either the top or bottom level of the space station wins.

$(37 + 84) \div (132 \div 12)$

$(17 \times 3.6) + (18 \times 2.4)$

36×25.3

29.84×16.5

$342.9 - 13.83$

$2647 + 8978$

99.8×60.2

225×226

0.68×15

$(6.8 \times 11.5) - (11.1 \times 6)$

$749.64 \div 12$

$463.94 - 186.3$

$1296 \div 54$

$8.7 \div 0.15$

$149.73 \div 69$

$8751 - 987$

65×1.68

$1908 \div 18$

$(96 \times 8) - (73 \times 7)$

13.7×11.9

$374.64 \div 14$

746×29

16×175.5

47×48

| 6007·96 | 11·6 | 109·2 | 11 | 26·76 | 910·8 | 10·2 | 106 | 104·4 | 329·07 | 7764 | 2808 |

| 62·47 | 2·17 | 50 850 | 163·03 | 24 | 277·64 | 58 | 257 | 21 634 | 11 625 | 492·36 | 2256 |

A Write in metres.

1 4·5 km
2 4·9 km
3 6·75 km
4 3·92 km
5 6·12 km   7 9·63 km
6 4·68 km   8 10·47 km

> 1 4·500 m

B Find how far each person has walked in kilometres.

9 Alice 2128 m
10 Jack 3604 m
11 Bill 63 m
12 Carmen 7628 m   13 Ethel 220 m

> 9 2·128 km

C Give each distance in metres.

14 4·27 km   18 0·302 km
15 3·906 km   19 3·206 km
16 17·659 km   20 4·03 km
17 0·007 km   21 6·5 km

D Measure each line to the nearest millimetre.

22 line 1 _____

23 line 2 _____

24 line 3 _____

25 line 4 _____

E Write each length.

26 line 1 in centimetres
27 line 4 in metres
28 line 3 in metres
29 line 2 in metres

F Space snails have snailometers. They show how many metres the snail has crawled in its lifetime. Find how far each snail has crawled to the nearest whole m and to the nearest $\frac{1}{10}$ m.

30 464·28 Slippy
32 264·96 Shelley
34 185·12 Sloppy

31 270·48 Slimy
33 417·62 Skiddy

Challenge ▭ ☒

Draw 10 dots on a sheet of paper. Label them 1 to 10. Measure to the nearest centimetre and then work out the new snailometer reading if:
a Slippy crawls from dot 2 to dot 8   **c** Shelley crawls from dot 5 to dot 1
b Skiddy crawls from dot 6 to dot 3   **d** Slimy crawls from dot 4 to dot 10.

Can you convert smaller units to larger and vice versa, m to km, cm or mm to m?

33

A Draw your own conversion graph for miles and kilometres. Make your graph as large as possible.

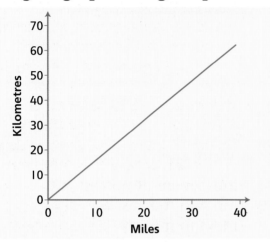

B Work out these distances as accurately as you can in kilometres. Use your graph.

1 Leeds 24 miles

2 Oxford 16½ miles

3 Cardiff 30 miles

4 Ayr 26½ miles

5 Dublin 12 miles

6 Dover 17½ miles

C Work out approximately how many miles away these towns are. Use your graph.

7 Gloucester 49 km

8 Holyhead 26 km

9 Aberdeen 13 km

10 Bembridge 29 km

11 Douglas 53 km

12 Slough 60 km

D Copy and complete this table. First, estimate each length showing clearly the units you are using. Next, measure each length. Write each length in metres rounded to the nearest 0·01 m.

	Estimate	Length (m)
13 length of your desk		
14 width of your chair		
15 length of your pencil		
16 width of a counter		

Challenge

Play with a partner. Use a ruler. Copy and complete this table. Choose 4 lengths to measure in the classroom. Measure the first in mm, the second and third in cm and the fourth in metres.

Both estimate each length. Measure each length. The closer estimate scores a point. The player with most points wins the game.

Length	Estimate	
	Me	My partner
	mm	mm
	cm	cm
	cm	cm
	m	m

Can you suggest suitable units and measuring equipment to estimate or measure length?

A This table shows time differences between London and some other places in the world.

Place	Time difference
Rio de Janeiro	− 3 hours
New York	− 5 hours
Los Angeles	− 8 hours
Cairo	+ 2 hours
Moscow	+ 3 hours
Karachi	+ 5 hours
Singapore	+ 8 hours
Sydney	+ 10 hours

Will Dial in London has to call someone at each place to wake them at 8:00 a.m. Find the time in London when he rings each place.

1 New York
2 Karachi
3 Cairo
4 Los Angeles
5 Singapore
6 Rio de Janeiro

7 Sydney
8 Moscow

1 1:00 p.m.

B Solve these problems.

9 Jake is allowed to watch TV for two hours. He watches two programmes for 40 minutes each and another for 15 minutes. How much viewing time has he left?

10 A dentist takes 25 minutes for a check-up and 35 minutes for a filling. If she works 8 hours a day, how much time will be left after 4 check-ups and 8 fillings?

11 Kevin walks 1 mile every 25 minutes. He leaves for a 6-mile walk at 14:20. At what time does he return?

A plane takes off at 09:00 and flies 550 miles every hour. It flies for 11 hours, lands for 2 hours 20 minutes to refuel and then flies for another $4\frac{1}{2}$ hours.

12 At what time does the journey end?
13 How far is the journey?

14 A shop opens for 55 hours per week. If it is open from 9:00 a.m. to 5:30 p.m. on Monday to Saturday, for how many hours does it open on Sunday?

Challenge   − ☐ ✕

Write the time in their own country when each person should call.
a Kylie in Sydney wants to ring Ivan in Moscow when it is 9:00 p.m. in Moscow.
b Scott in Los Angeles wants to ring Neela in Karachi when it is 3:00 p.m. in Karachi.
c Yusef in Cairo wants to ring Lucy in London when it is noon in London.
d Carrie in New York wants to ring Li in Singapore when it is 23:00 in Singapore.

A Plot these points on cm-squared paper. Join them in order with straight lines. Name the shape you find.

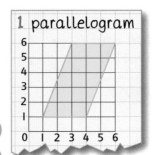

1 parallelogram

1 (1,1) (4,1) (6,6) (3,6) (1,1)

2 (7,1) (7,6) (2,6) (2,1) (7,1)

3 (0,0) (3,6) (6,0) (0,0)

4 (0,2) (0,5) (4,6) (4,0) (0,2)

5 (⁻2,1) (⁻2,5) (2,5) (⁻2,1)

6 (⁻4,2) (⁻7,0) (⁻4,⁻6) (⁻1,0) (⁻4,2)

7 (1,⁻4) (4,⁻4) (4,2) (1,2) (1,⁻4)

8 (⁻2,6) (2,6) (5,2) (2,⁻3) (⁻4,⁻2) (⁻5,4) (⁻2,6)

B Give 4 points that could be the positions of vertices of these shapes.

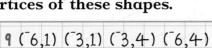

9 (⁻6,1) (⁻3,1) (⁻3,4) (⁻6,4)

9 a square in the second quadrant
10 a trapezium in the third quadrant
11 a parallelogram in the fourth quadrant
12 a heptagon in the second quadrant

C A square has 2 of its vertices at (2,⁻3) and (1,⁻2).

13 On a grid draw 3 different squares that have these points as 2 of their vertices.
14 Give the coordinates of the 4 vertices of each square you have drawn.

D Copy this trapezium on a grid. Translate the trapezium:

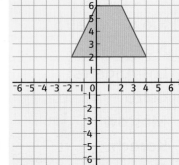

15 ⁺3 in the x direction
16 ⁻6 in the y direction
17 ⁻6 in the x direction and ⁺1 in the y direction
18 ⁻4 in the x direction and ⁻8 in the y direction.

Challenge

You need a partner, 20 counters, a grid on cm-squared paper showing all four quadrants numbered from ⁻4 to 4 on both the x and y axes and 2 sets of 9 cards numbered from ⁻4 to 4. Place the 20 counters on any 20 different points on the grid. Shuffle each set of cards and place them face down in a pile. The first set are the x-axis numbers. The second set are the y-axis numbers. Take turns to turn over the top card of each pile to give the coordinates of a point on the grid. If there is a counter at this point, take it. Shuffle the cards once both packs are used. The first to collect 5 counters is the winner.

Can you read and plot points beyond the first quadrant?

A Solve these problems. For each, write down your calculation. Estimate first.

1 A roll of fabric is 10 m long. Two customers each buy a length of $2\frac{1}{2}$ m, and another customer buys 135 cm of fabric. How much fabric is left on the roll?

2 After 10 minutes in a 5 km race, Seb has run 1·75 km and Ashley has run 925 m. In the next 10 minutes Ashley stops for a rest and Seb runs another 1·4 km. How far behind Seb is Ashley now?

3 Passengers can take 20 kg of luggage onto a plane. Stu Ward has two bags weighing 14·85 kg and 950 g. How much more weight can Stu take on board?

4 Paving slabs are 58 cm long. When a path is laid, a gap of 8 mm is left between slabs. How far will the path stretch after 12 slabs are laid?

An airline has 4210 seats available every day. How many seats are available:

5 in one week

6 in June

7 in a leap year?

8 How many 125 mm lengths of plastic can be cut from a strip measuring 4·375 m?

9 To get to work, John walks for 18 minutes to reach the station. The train journey takes 3 times as long. He then walks to his office for a quarter of an hour. How long does his journey take?

10 Abi runs 350 m. Anish runs 3·15 km. How many times further than Abi has Anish run?

Challenge

a Copy and complete this conversion graph for kilograms and pounds (1 kg ≈ 2·2 pounds) onto a large sheet of squared paper.

b Work out the approximate mass in pounds of each item in Mr Bargain's shopping bag.

apples 8·5 kg	mushrooms 500 g
carrots 2·6 kg	bananas 4·25 kg
potatoes 9·5 kg	charcoal 12 kg

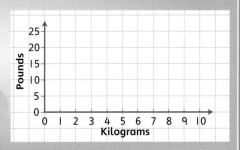

c Find the mass in kg of 5 items in your classroom. Work out each mass in pounds.

Can you solve story problems involving km, m, cm, mm, minutes and hours and explain and record how the problem was solved?

37

A Write approximately how many litres for each.

1 3 gallons
2 2½ gallons
3 8 gallons

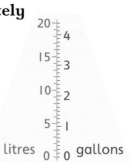

B There are 8 pints in a gallon. Write approximately how many pints of petrol for each.

4 10 litres
5 18 litres
6 40 litres

C Find approximately how many centimetres.

3 feet = 1 yard
12 inches = 1 foot
1 inch ≈ 2·5 cm

7 10 inches
8 18 inches
9 2½ feet
10 2 yards 1 foot
11 1 yard 2 feet 3 inches

D Find approximately how many inches.

12 20 cm
13 35 cm
14 1 m
15 0·6 m

E Find a situation when you might measure in these units.

16 millilitres | 16 taking medicine
17 grams
18 kilometres
19 litres
20 millimetres
21 kilograms

F These scales measure in kg. Work out the approximate mass shown by each arrow.

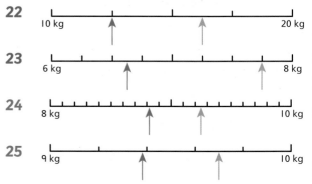

22
23
24
25

G For each description, find an object in the classroom.

26 more than 8 inches long but less than 1 foot
27 heavier than 1 pound but lighter than 1 kg
28 a capacity of more than half a pint but less than 1 litre
29 a width of more than 6 inches but less than ¼ m

Challenge

a Work out your weight in pounds.
b Work out your height in feet and inches.
c Work out your span in inches.
d Work out the length of your classroom in yards, feet and inches.
e Work out approximately how many millilitres of milk a pint bottle will hold (1l ≈ 1·75 pints).

38

Can you read measuring scales and convert imperial units to the equivalent metric unit?

Copy this grid twice onto cm-squared paper.

Follow each set of instructions to draw two shapes.

Start with the first point and join each point with a straight line to the point which follows.

Answer these questions.

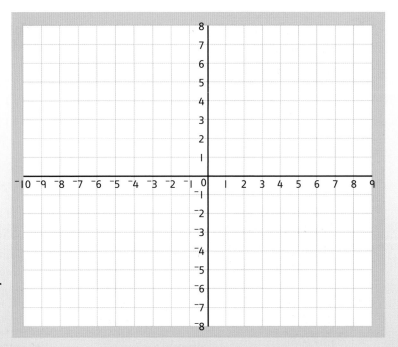

1 Which shape is the Eiffel Tower?

2 What is the outer perimeter of each shape?

3 What area on your grid is enclosed by each shape?

Shape 1

($^-$3,$^-$1) (0,$^-$1) (1,0) (1,1) (0,2) ($^-$1,2) ($^-$2,1) ($^-$2,0) ($^-$1,$^-$1) (2,$^-$1) (2,7) (7,7)
(7,3) (6,3) (6,6) (5,6) (5,3) (4,3) (4,6) (3,6) (3,3) ($^-$3,3) ($^-$3,7) ($^-$8,7) ($^-$8,3)
($^-$7,3) ($^-$7,6) ($^-$6,6) ($^-$6,3) ($^-$5,3) ($^-$5,6) ($^-$4,6) ($^-$4,3) ($^-$3,3) ($^-$3,$^-$8) ($^-$10,$^-$8)
($^-$10,$^-$4) ($^-$7,$^-$2) ($^-$4,$^-$4) ($^-$10,$^-$4) ($^-$10,2) ($^-$9,1) ($^-$9,2) ($^-$8,3) ($^-$8,1) ($^-$6,2)
($^-$4,1) ($^-$4,3) ($^-$4,$^-$8) ($^-$2,$^-$8) ($^-$2,$^-$5) ($^-$1,$^-$3) (0,$^-$3) (1,$^-$5) (1,$^-$8) (9,$^-$8) (9,$^-$4)
(6,$^-$2) (3,$^-$4) (9,$^-$4) (9,$^-$2) (8,$^-$1) (8,2) (7,3) (7,1) (5,2) (3,1) (3,3) (3,$^-$8)
(2,$^-$8) (2,$^-$1) (7,$^-$1) (7,3) ($^-$8,3) ($^-$8,$^-$1) ($^-$3,$^-$1)

Shape 2

($^-$10,0) ($^-$9,0) ($^-$9,1) ($^-$7,1) (1,2) (1,$^-$2) ($^-$7,$^-$1) ($^-$7,1) ($^-$8,0) ($^-$7,$^-$1)
($^-$8,$^-$1) ($^-$7,0) ($^-$8,1) ($^-$8,$^-$1) ($^-$9,$^-$1) ($^-$9,0) ($^-$8,0) (4,1) (4,3) (6,3)
(4,2) (6,2) (4,1) (6,1) (4,0) (6,0) (4,$^-$1) (6,$^-$1) (4,$^-$2) (6,$^-$2) (4,$^-$3)
(6,$^-$3) (6,$^-$4) (8,$^-$6) (8,$^-$3) (6,$^-$4) (6,$^-$2) (8,$^-$6) (8,$^-$3) (6,$^-$2) (6,2)
(8,6) (6,4) (8,3) (6,2) (6,4) (8,6) (8,$^-$6) (6,$^-$4) (4,$^-$3) (4,1) (4,$^-$3)
(1,$^-$2) (2,$^-$1) (1,0) (2,1) (1,2) (4,3) (6,4) (6,$^-$1) (4,$^-$1) ($^-$8,0)

A **Answer these. Show your working.**

1   383 + 218
2   637 + 486
3   945 − 819
4   715 − 566
5   1027 + 4378

6   1605 + 897
7   4360 − 1751
8   3247 − 868
9   9006 − 1623

B **Follow these steps to answer the questions.**

> **a**   estimate the answer
> **b**   work out the answer and show your working
> **c**   write **H** if you worked out the answer in your head,
>   **P** if you used pencil and paper,
>   **C** if you used a calculator

10   6002 − 4994
11   3025 − 1826
12   467 + 854
13   3774 + 8405

14   7216 − 3982
15   749 + 857
16   903 − 468
17   9000 − 3659

C **Answer these. Use a column method.**

18   32·6 − 11·9
19   115 − 62·8
20   106 − 46·39

21   6·34 + 8·57
22   726 − 137·24
23   62·8 + 74·96

D **Solve these problems.**

24   Dipti dived to a depth of 12·6 m, Scubi dived to a depth of 33·9 m. How much deeper did Scubi dive than Dipti?

25   A yacht travelled 69·2 km. A cruiser travelled 102·75 km further. How far did the cruiser travel?

26   In the snail race, Slimy slithered 26·3 cm and Michelle slithered 41·17 cm. How much further did Michelle slither than Slimy?

27   Baby Jones has built a tower of bricks 78 cm tall. Baby Patel has added 3 more bricks, each 90 mm high. How tall is the tower now?

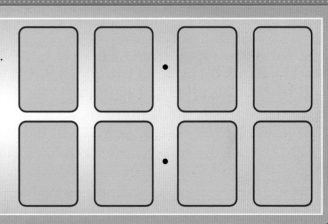

Challenge

Play with a partner. Use number cards 0 to 9 and a large copy of this grid. In turn, shuffle the cards and deal out 8 of them on your grid to create 2 decimal numbers.
Subtract the smaller number from the larger number. The player with the larger difference scores a point.
The first to 5 points wins the game.

Can you use written methods of column addition and subtraction for numbers involving decimals?

A Write 2 numbers that make each total.

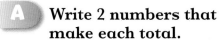
1 6·9, 7·8

1	14·7	4	100·7	7	13·63
2	16·3	5	91·6	8	11·95
3	20·2	6	18·75		

B Write 2 numbers for each difference.

9 19, 5·5

9	13·5	12	8·6	15	4·55
10	11·2	13	9·8	16	3·26
11	4·9	14	6·25		

C Solve these problems. Check each answer.

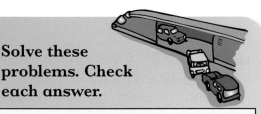

Train Fares			
Car up to 4 m	£80·45	Minibus	£130·80
Car longer		Vehicle driver	free
than 4 m	£120·75	Passengers: Adult	£13·25
Van	£110·50	Child	£6·55

What is the difference in cost between the fares for:

17 a van and a car less than 4 m?
18 a minibus and a car longer than 4 m?

Find each total cost.

19 a car less than 4 m with a driver and 2 adult passengers
20 a minibus with a driver and 12 adult passengers
21 a family of 2 adults and 2 children in a car longer than 4 m
22 a van with a driver and an adult passenger
23 a minibus with 10 adults
24 4 adults pay a total of £160·50. In what sort of vehicle are they travelling?
25 A group of 4 adults and their children travel in a van and a minibus. They pay a total of £300·55. How many children are travelling?

Challenge

Bus fares are £1·75 for adults and 90p for children. Every time the bus crosses into another colour zone, adults pay an extra 55p and children an extra 30p.
For example, Mr Fide travels from Fulton to Malton. He crosses into 2 new zones and pays £2·85.
Work out these costs.

a 1 adult and 2 children travelling from Dill to Fulton
b 1 adult and 1 child travelling from Dill to Grays
c 4 adults travelling from Lock to Drew
d Mrs Comfort pays £11·70 to take her family from Grays to Nanton. If there are 2 adults, how many children are there?

Make up 5 questions for a partner to solve.

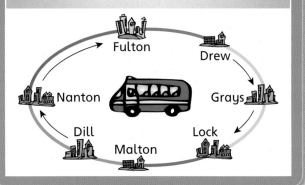

Can you choose the appropriate operations to solve word problems?

41

A Each answer is wrong. Explain how you know this without using a calculator or working out the answer.

1 answer must end in a 0

1 $364 \times 10 = 3644$
2 $45 \times 85 = 3820$
3 $4758 - 1963 = 3795$
4 $64 \times 7 = 442$
5 $18 \times 50 = 950$
6 $37 \times 26 = 9620$
7 $188 \div 8 = 235$

B Answer these. Use a calculator.

8 $\bullet \times 3.75 = 97.5$
9 $63.8 - \ast = 33.9$
10 $0.08 \times \blacksquare = 1.72$
11 $\ast + 18.6 = 29.85$
12 $\bullet \times 3.62 = 56.11$

C Write the inverse operation for each. Check the answers using a calculator. Which answers are wrong?

13 $6.3 \times 4.5 = 28.45$
14 $9.6 \div 5 = 1.92$
15 $3.28 \times 2.5 = 9.2$
16 $13.54 \times 65 = 880.01$
17 $1496.38 - 259.67 = 1263.71$
18 $8406.37 + 996.48 = 9402.85$

13 $28.45 \div 4.5 \approx 6.32$ answer is wrong

D Give an approximate answer for each. Say if the answer will be larger or smaller than your approximation.

19 4.6×19
20 $955.5 \div 245$
21 $548.76 + 196.38$
22 5.8×1.9
23 $(56.6 \times 3.8) \div (152 \div 8)$
24 $(4.8 \times 5.2) + (6.9 \times 7.7)$
25 $(47.36 + 12.28) \times (1.75 \times 12)$
26 $(83.95 \div 4.6) \times (11.68 + 14.32)$

Challenge — □ ×

Play with a partner. Use 2 sets of counters.
Choose any pink number. Multiply it or divide it by any purple number. If your answer is on the grid, cover it with a counter. The first player with 3 counters in one column wins the game.

19.68	47.56	23.6
10.88	8.6	41.75
26.6	44.55	16.4

1.5	25	2.8
1.45	3.8	1.65	4.25
4.3		2.05	2.56

27	29.7	43.89	114.38	169.29
1.67	2.56	9.6	32.8	23.78
158.65	24.08	202.13	13.12	14.19
12.47	215	34.22	4.25	106.88
70.52	36.55	116.9	38.94	8

42

Can you calculate by doing the inverse operation using a calculator?

A Write the terms missing from each sequence.

1 15, 21, ★, ★, ★, 45
2 5, 16, ●, ●, 49
3 47, ●, ●, 23, 15
4 14, 7, ●, ●, ⁻14
5 ⁻20, ⁻12, ●, ●, 12

B Write the missing numbers in each sequence. Explain the rule.

6 19, 26, 33, ◖, ◖, ◖
7 4, 12, 20, ▲, ▲, ▲
8 50, 41, 32, ◆, ◆, ◆
9 26, 38, 50, ✹, ✹, ✹
10 1, 2, 3, 5, ◆, ◆, ◆

C Write the tenth term in the sequence.

11 in question 6   13 in question 9
12 in question 8   14 in question 10

D Copy and complete these sequences. Write the rule.

15 6·4, 6·6, 6·8, ●, ●, ●, ●, ●
16 1·25, 1·5, 1·75, ■, ■, ■, ■
17 9·25, 8·75, 8·25, ●, ●, ●, ●
18 1·25, 1, 0·75, ◆, ◆, ◆, ◆
19 10·7, 10·4, 10·1, ★, ★, ★, ★
20 1·3, 0·9, 0·5, ✹, ✹, ✹, ✹

E Write the eighth term counting upwards in each sequence.

21 the start number is 4 and the steps are 6

  | 21 4·6 |

22 the start number is 3 and the steps are 9
23 the start number is 12 and the steps are 10
24 the start number is 0 and the steps are 11
25 the start number is ⁻9 and the steps are 6

Challenge

Play with a partner. Use a dice and a score sheet. Each set of numbers is part of a sequence. Work through each sequence in turn as follows.

a Roll the dice. The dice number tells you which term is in the yellow box.
b Work out the 10th term in the sequence. This is your score for the sequence.
c Your partner now takes a turn.

d Each add together your 7 scores. The higher total wins the game.

For example: 2 , 9, 16, 23... [dice], so
2 is the 5th term in the sequence.
The 10th term is 37. Score 37.

A 2 , 9, 16, 23   E 1·2 , 1·7, 2·2, 2·7
B ⁻6 , ⁻1, 4, 9   F 114·25 , 114·75,
C 158 ,147, 136, 125   115·25, 115·75
D 0 , 2·5, 5, 7·5   G 96 , 104, 112, 120

A Find how many counters there will be in the tenth term of each sequence.

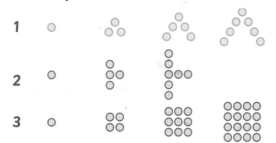

1

2

3

4

B Copy and complete each table to show how each number sequence extends.

5

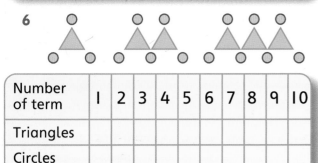

Number of term	1	2	3	4	5	6	7	8	9	10
Squares	1	2								
Circles	4									

6

Number of term	1	2	3	4	5	6	7	8	9	10
Triangles										
Circles										

C Look at the sequence in question 5.

7 Find how many circles there will be in the 30th term.

8 Find how many squares there will be in the 100th term.

9 Find how many circles there will be in the nth term.

10 Write a formula for the number of circles in the nth term.

D Look at the sequence in question 6.

11 Find how many triangles there will be in the 20th term.

12 Find how many circles there will be in the 200th term.

13 Find how many circles there are in the nth term.

14 Write a formula for the number of circles in the nth term.

Challenge ▢✕

Write a formula for the number of counters in the nth term of each sequence.

a

b

c

d

Can you express a relationship in symbols and use a simple formula?

A Copy and complete these tables. Write the rule for each sequence in words.

1

Number of term	1	2	3	4	5	6	10	50	100
Number of counters	3	5	7	9	11				

2

Number of term	1	2	3	4	5	6	10	50	100
Number of counters	2	5	8	11					

3

Number of term	1	2	3	4	5	6	10	200	1000
Number of counters	5	7	9	11					

B Write a formula for the nth term of the sequence.

4 in question 1   **6** in question 3
5 in question 2

C If the formula for the nth term in a sequence is nth term = 3n + 2, find these.

7 8th term   **9** 500th term
8 25th term

D If the formula for the nth term in a sequence is nth term = 5n − 2, find these.

10 9th term   **12** 100th term
11 50th term

E If the formula for the nth term in a sequence is nth term = 7n + 4, find these.

13 8th term   **15** 111th term
14 55th term

F In a snooker tournament each player must play every other player. Find how many matches must be played for each number.

16 3 players   **20** 15 players
17 5 players   **21** 20 players
18 8 players
19 10 players

World Long-sighted Snooker Tournament

Challenge   — ☐ ✕

2 lines crossing each other intersect at 1 point.

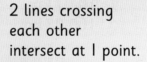

3 lines all crossing each other intersect at 3 points.

Draw a diagram to show 4 lines all crossing each other. Remember, every line must cross all of the other lines. How many points of intersection do you find?

Work out how many points of intersection there will be when:
a 5 lines all cross each other
b 6 lines all cross each other
c 10 lines all cross each other
d 15 lines all cross each other.

A   Work out the perimeter of each shape.

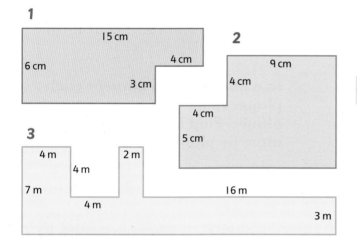

1

15 cm
6 cm
4 cm
3 cm

2

9 cm
4 cm
4 cm
5 cm

3

4 m
4 m
2 m
7 m
4 m
16 m
3 m

B   Find how many metres.

4	5·36 km	8	3·75 km
5	4·98 km	9	10·07 km
6	3·06 km	10	100·03 km
7	4·9 km		

C   Find how many kilometres.

11	6327 m	15	495 m
12	4031 m	16	6940 m
13	2000 m	17	202 m
14	4006 m		

D   A quadrilateral has vertices at (3,1) (0,4) (3,5) and (4,2).

18 Draw the quadrilateral on a grid.

19 Translate the quadrilateral $^+4$ in the x direction.

20 Translate the quadrilateral $^-2$ in the x direction and $^+6$ in the y direction.

E   Answer these. Use a column method.

21   45·7 − 16·9   24   9·73 + 4·98

22   124 − 18·7   25   736 − 149·7

23   108·1 − 37·6

F   Answer these. Use a calculator.

26   ⬤ × 9·25 = 148

27   66·2 − △ = 38·7

28   0·08 × ◖ = 4·32

29   ⬤ + 37·85 = 42·6

30   4·76 × 18·5 = ⬤

31   ⬣ ÷ 8 = 5·46

G   Copy and complete these sequences. Write the rule.

32   4·9, 5·6, 6·3, ⬤, ⬤, ⬤, ⬤, ⬤

33   4·75, 4·25, 3·75, ✳, ✳, ✳, ✳, ✳

34   1·6, 1·2, 0·8, ⬤, ⬤, ⬤, ⬤, ⬤

35   76·5, 67·5, 58·5, ▲, ▲, ▲, ▲, ▲

H   Write a formula for the number of counters in the nth term of each sequence.

36

37

38   ●●   ●●●●   ●●●●●●

A Write in order, smallest first.

1	3·27	3·12	3·71	3·21	3·72
2	4·75	5·47	4·57	7·54	4·45
3	5·91	5·19	5·11	5·99	5·01
4	6·02	6·22	6·26	6·12	6·21
5	11·68	6·18	8·16	6·66	6·68

B Round to the nearest integer.

6 4·23
7 5·71
8 8·67

6 4

9 4·65   11 12·49
10 11·55   12 6·84

C Write in order, coldest first.

13 6 °C   ⁻2 °C   8 °C   0 °C   ⁻7 °C
14 ⁻4 °C   ⁻11 °C   1 °C   6 °C   ⁻5 °C
15 ⁻16 °C   ⁻20 °C   ⁻12 °C   ⁻0 °C   4 °C
16 ⁻8 °C   ⁻7 °C   ⁻10 °C   2 °C   ⁻12 °C
17 9 °C   ⁻8 °C   7 °C   4 °C   ⁻5 °C

D Find each new temperature.

18 the temperature is ⁻2 °C
    and falls by 5 degrees
19 the temperature is 4 °C
    and falls by 7 degrees
20 the temperature is ⁻4 °C
    and rises by 8 degrees
21 the temperature is ⁻16 °C
    and rises by 7 degrees
22 the temperature is ⁻3 °C
    and falls by 12 degrees

E Answer these. Use a calculator.

23 6 − 8   28 16 − 24
24 ⁻4 + 7   29 ⁻6 − 9
25 ⁻14 + 24   30 ⁻14 − 7
26 ⁻4 + 17   31 ⁻10 + 32
27 ⁻9 + 11   32 ⁻14 − 30

Challenge ⊟☒

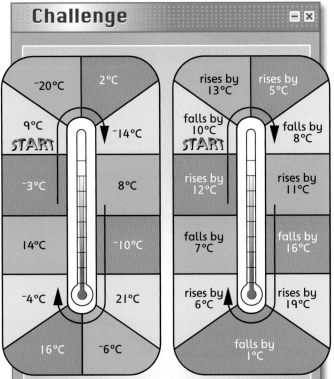

Play with a partner. Use 2 sets of 4
counters and a dice. Both place a
counter on START on each track.
Take turns to roll the dice to give
your move for both tracks. This gives
you a temperature. For example, ⁻3 °C
falls 8 degrees, becomes ⁻11 °C.
The player with the higher
temperature scores a point. The first
to 10 points wins the game.

Can you use negative numbers in the context of temperatures?

47

A Copy and complete this bank statement.

Mr Sven Dallot

	Date	Money out	Money in	Balance
	1st Jan			£130
	2nd Jan	£142		⁻£12
1	3rd Jan		£50	
2	4th Jan	£37		
3	7th Jan	£260		
4	8th Jan	£140	£20	
5	9th Jan		£500	
6	10th Jan	£371·50		

B Write the value of the red number.

7 6·84 10 0·35 $7 \frac{4}{100}$
8 3·73 11 8·37
9 4·98 12 10·63 13 6·26

C Write in order, shortest first.

14 3·62 m 3·02 m 3·06 m 3·26 m 2·36 m
15 4·99 m 5·11 m 5·01 m 4·95 m 4·59 m
16 11·01 m 11·1 m 10·11 m 10·01 m 10·1 m

D Copy and complete.

17 $\frac{4}{100} = \frac{}{1000}$ 19 $\frac{10}{100} = \frac{}{1000}$ 21 $\frac{20}{100} = \frac{}{1000}$
18 $\frac{9}{100} = \frac{}{1000}$ 20 $\frac{8}{100} = \frac{}{1000}$

E Write each number as a decimal.

22 1 tenth, 3 hundredths and 9 thousandths | 22 0·139
23 4 tenths and 6 thousandths
24 3 hundredths and 7 thousandths
25 23 thousandths
26 120 thousandths

Challenge

Play with a partner. Use a dice, number cards 0 to 9 and a large copy of the grid below. Roll the dice to select your tortoise.

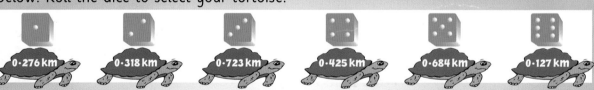

0·276 km 0·318 km 0·723 km 0·425 km 0·684 km 0·127 km

In turn, shuffle the cards and deal the top 3 in order onto the grid.
Add the grid distance to your tortoise distance.
The player whose tortoise has travelled the furthest total distance scores a point. The first to 5 points wins the game.

0·☐☐☐ km

 Can you answer questions such as 'What does the digit 6 in 4·236 represent?'

A Write in order, smallest first.

1 0·126   0·613   0·895   0·237
2 0·375   0·861   0·324   0·165
3 0·223   0·232   0·322   0·332
4 0·717   0·071   0·171   0·017
5 0·372   0·327   0·371   0·312

B Write a decimal fraction with a value between each pair.

6 0·163 and 0·171
7 0·204 and 0·209
8 0·312 and 0·317
9 0·065 and 0·071
10 0·732 and 0·742
11 0·699 and 0·703
12 0·099 and 0·101
13 0·606 and 0·611

6 0·169

C Round to the nearest tenth.

14 3·46   17 8·09
15 3·72   18 11·67
16 4·81   19 13·49   20 15·55

14 3·5

D Round to the nearest whole metre.

21 14·58 m   23 16·28 m   25 16·48 m
22 18·37 m   24 47·81 m   26 11·19 m

E From each set choose the decimal number equivalent to each fraction.

27 $\frac{263}{1000}$ 2·63   26·3   0·263   1·263
28 $\frac{47}{1000}$ 0·047   0·47   4·7   0·147
29 $\frac{623}{1000}$ 6·23   0·623   62·3   6·203
30 $\frac{109}{1000}$ 0·19   1·09   10·9   0·109

F Write in order, smallest first.

31 4·53   4·352   4·52   4·235
32 6·041 6·41   6·4   6·141 6·144
33 0·963 0·69   0·693   1·69   0·936
34 11·01 10·111 10·011 10·01   11·11
35 72·43 72·344 72·4   73   73·424
36 6·804 6·48   6·048   6·884 6·448

G Round to the nearest hundredth, the nearest tenth and the nearest whole number.

37 8·637
38 2·456
39 3·027
40 16·552   42 18·694
41 13·255   43 3·555

37 8·64, 8·6, 9

:::: Challenge ::::::::::::::::::::::::::::: — □ ×

Work with a partner. Use suitable measuring equipment.
a Measure your heights to the nearest 0·01 m.
b Measure the width of your table to the nearest 10 cm and to the nearest 0·01 m.
c Measure the length of your classroom to the nearest metre and to the nearest 10 cm.
d Measure the capacity of a container to the nearest 10 ml.

Can you order a mixed set of numbers with up to 3 decimal places?

49

A Find which colour rocket carries the answer to each question.

1 yellow

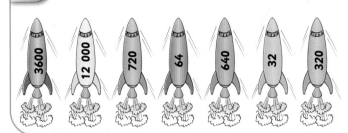

3600   12 000   720   64   640   32   320

1   600 × 20
2   6400 ÷ 100
3   double 360
4   half of 1440
5   40 × 90
6   3200 ÷ 100
7   400 × 30
8   10 × ✸ = 320
9   100 × ▢ = 6400
10 32 000 ÷ 1000
11 half of 640

B Find the exact answer. Show your working. Estimate first. Write Ⓗ if you worked out the answer in your head.

12   4·23 × 10
13   6·89 × 100
14   4·25 × 5
15   9·26 × 500
16   4·69 × 1000
17   6·48 × 50
18   46·3 × 4
19   5·8 × 6
20   0·55 × 2
21   4·15 × 8
22   6·892 × 100
23   3·726 × 1000
24   38 ÷ 10
25   4·591 × 10
26   4·6 ÷ 100
27   490 ÷ 100
28   68 ÷ 1000
29   double 1·45
30   double 6·324
31   29 ÷ 1000

Challenge ▬ ✕

Play with a partner. Use 2 sets of 7 counters and a calculator.

18	163	189	1·98
115	0·62	18·9	1800
0·18	0·85	0·198	8·5
6·2	1767	177·6	1150

Take turns to choose one of the questions below. Work out the answer. Check your answer with a calculator. If your answer is on the grid, cover it with a counter.
The first to have 3 counters in a straight line wins the game.

62 ÷ 100	12·4 ÷ 2	2·25 × 8
180 ÷ 1000	1·89 × 100	19·8 ÷ 100
0·33 × 6	18000 ÷ 10	44·4 × 4
1·767 × 1000	3·26 × 50	2·3 × 500
1·15 × 100	85 ÷ 100	425 ÷ 50
	2·1 × 9	

Can you multiply or divide a decimal fraction by 10, 100 or 1000?

A Write 3 facts linked to each number statement.

1 4·4 × 7 = 30·8
2 6·3 × 7 = 44·1
3 4·8 × 4 = 19·2
4 9·8 × 7 = 68·6
5 19·3 × 5 = 96·5
6 27·4 × 8 = 219·2
7 66·6 × 9 = 599·4

> 1 7 × 4·4 = 30·8
> 30·8 ÷ 7 = 4·4
> 30·8 ÷ 4·4 = 7

B Answer these. Give each quotient as a fraction.

8 64 ÷ 7
9 53 ÷ 10
10 69 ÷ 8
11 46 ÷ 5
12 33 ÷ 4

13 71 ÷ 2
14 103 ÷ 9

> 8 $9\frac{1}{7}$

C Change to decimal fractions. Use a calculator.

15 $\frac{1}{4}$
16 $\frac{1}{8}$
17 $\frac{3}{8}$

18 $\frac{3}{4}$
19 $\frac{9}{20}$
20 $\frac{5}{8}$

21 $\frac{3}{20}$
22 $\frac{7}{8}$
23 $\frac{11}{50}$

D Answer these. Give each quotient as a decimal fraction.

24 65 ÷ 4
25 55 ÷ 4
26 47 ÷ 5
27 86 ÷ 10
28 42 ÷ 8

29 63 ÷ 5
30 83 ÷ 8
31 39 ÷ 10
32 47 ÷ 8
33 52 ÷ 20
34 147 ÷ 8

> 24 16·25

E Round the quotients to 1 decimal place.

35 423 ÷ 8
36 327 ÷ 8
37 163 ÷ 4
38 101 ÷ 8

39 321 ÷ 4
40 76 ÷ 5
41 95 ÷ 8
42 51 ÷ 20
43 103 ÷ 20

> 35 52·9

F Check each answer using the inverse operation. Correct any wrong answers.

44 149 ÷ 5 = 29·8
45 323 ÷ 8 = 40·125
46 515 ÷ 4 = 128·25
47 367 ÷ 8 = 45·875
48 211 ÷ 5 = 44·2
49 379 ÷ 20 = 18·59

Challenge

Play with a partner. Use 2 sets of 9 counters, 3 dice and a calculator.

0·8	0·5	0·25	0·75	0·4	0·5	0·75	0·5
0·125	0·375	0·6	0·375	0·625	0·25	0·2	0·875

Take turns to roll the 3 dice to form a 3-digit number. Choose to divide your number by 4, 5 or 8. Write the remainder as a decimal fraction.
E.g. 365 ÷ 8 = 45·625, r = 0·625
If this remainder shows in a box, cover it with a counter. You can place only 1 counter at each turn. The first with 3 counters in any box wins the game.

Can you express a quotient as a fraction or decimal fraction?

51

A Answer to the nearest whole number and also to one decimal place. Use a calculator.

1 34 , 34·1

1   $307 \div 9$ 3 $324 \div 7$ 5 $329 \div 23$
2   $461 \div 3$ 4 $816 \div 18$ 6 $411 \div 16$

B Find the answers to the nearest whole number and to one decimal place. Estimate first. Check your answers and show your working.

7   $527 \div 18$ 9 $543 \div 29$ 11 $427 \div 15$
8   $345 \div 19$ 10 $511 \div 13$ 12 $573 \div 49$

C Solve each problem. Show your working.

13   Ann Tarctic has saved £7,000 for a family cruise. If tickets cost £1217 each, how many tickets can she buy?

14   Photo albums hold 65 photographs. How many albums will be needed for 517 photographs?

15   19 concert tickets cost £242·25. What is the cost of each ticket?

16   It costs £6177 to take 29 children on a trip. What is the cost for each child?

17   Tickets for a theme park cost £17 for adults and half price for children. 4 adults have £100. How many children can they take?

18   If a theatre holds 515 people and is full for every performance, how many performances will have been given when 1 million people have seen the show?

Challenge   — ×

Write a calculation that will give an answer with a whole number and a remainder equivalent to:

a   0·5   d   0·25
b   0·75   e   0·8   g   0·7
c   0·2   f   0·3   h   0·125

Write a division question that gives the answer:

i   6·4   l   8·75
j   3·2   m   11·8
k   5·25   n   20·62

A Answer these. Use factors to find 2 different numbers with the same product.

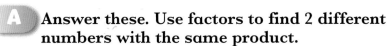

1	24 × 18	4	40 × 36	7	42 × 14	9	88 × 8
2	16 × 32	5	64 × 24	8	30 × 56	10	72 × 12
3	28 × 18	6	12 × 48				

```
1        24 × 18 = 432
    6 × 4 × 6 × 3 = 432
    6 × 6 × 4 × 3 = 432
        36 × 12 = 432
```

B Answer these.

11 $6 \times (4 + 7)$ 13 $(16 + 15) \times 3$ 15 $49 + (12 \times 4)$

12 $(4 \times 9) + 11$ 14 $(64 \div 8) + 27$ 16 $(4 \times 12) \div 8$

17 $(81 \div 9) \times 11$

C Give two possible solutions for each missing number.

```
18  50 − (4 × 3) = 38
    50 − (2 × 6) = 38
```

18 $50 - (\blacksquare \times \blacksquare) = 38$

19 $(\blacksquare + 4) \times \blacktriangleleft = 60$

20 $9 \times (\maltese - \blacksquare) = 99$

21 $(80 - \blacksquare) \times (40 - \blacksquare) = 20$

22 $(\maltese - 16) + \blacksquare = 31$

23 $120 - (\blacktriangleleft - \maltese) = 60$

24 $6 \times (\blacksquare + 3) \times \blacksquare = 120$

D Work out the missing number. Check each answer using the inverse operation.

25 $630 \div \blacksquare = 15.75$

26 $\maltese \div 52 = 12.25$

27 $693 \div \blacksquare = 15.4$

28 $\blacktriangleleft \times 5.5 = 198$

29 $\maltese \times 55 = 312.4$

30 $49.25 \times \blacksquare = 1132.75$

31 $(\blacksquare \times 6) + 5.9 = 19.7$

32 $6 \times (3.5 + \blacksquare) \times 4 = 292.8$

33 $120 \div (3.2 + \blacksquare) = 25$

Challenge

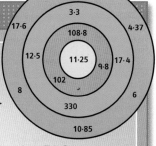

Take turns to choose a question. Place a counter next to it. Find your answer on the target. Score 10 for yellow, 6 for pink, 3 for green, 1 for orange. Highest score after all questions are answered wins.

○ $6 \times (9 + 8)$

○ $\maltese \times (9 + 8) = 102$

○ $250 \div 20$

○ $783 \div 45$

○ 36×9

○ 12.8×8.5

○ $\blacksquare \div 40 = 8.25$

○ $418.88 \div 52.36$

○ $450 \div 40$

○ $\maltese \times 8 = 86.8$

○ $(\blacktriangleleft + 9.5) \times 6 = 76.8$

○ $490 \div 50$

○ $\blacksquare \times 3.7 = 65.12$

○ $\bullet \times 32 = 139.84$

Target values: 324, 3·3, 17·6, 108·8, 4·37, 12·5, 11·25, 17·4, 9·8, 102, 8, 6, 330, 10·85

A Use a chunking method to find the exact answer. Estimate first.

1 347 ÷ 7
2 422 ÷ 5
3 691 ÷ 8
4 515 ÷ 3
5 743 ÷ 6
6 437 ÷ 4
7 843 ÷ 9

```
1  7)347
     -280  (40 × 7)
      67
     -63  (9 × 7)
       4
   Answer  49 r 4
```

B Give each answer as a mixed number. Use a method of short division.

8 295 ÷ 4
9 368 ÷ 6
10 508 ÷ 7
11 633 ÷ 8
12 541 ÷ 4
13 263 ÷ 6
14 453 ÷ 9

```
8        7 3 r 3
    4)2 9 5
   Answer 73 3/4
```

15 604 ÷ 5
16 371 ÷ 8
17 767 ÷ 3

C Solve each problem. Use a method of short division. Check each answer by using the inverse operation.

18 4 tickets for a concert cost £46. What is the cost of each ticket?

19 3 people share the cost of a holiday. If the holiday costs £931·50 in total, how much does each person pay?

20 Kai Yak is paying $\frac{1}{8}$ of the cost of a boat. If the boat costs £842, how much does Kai pay?

21 7 people share a prize of £234·50. How much does each person receive?

22 If you eat early you get $\frac{1}{3}$ off the price of a meal. How much will you save on a meal costing £56·25?

23 5 fans buy tickets for a football match. If they pay £107·60 altogether, what is the cost of each ticket?

Challenge

Follow the correct answers. Where is the ship sailing to?

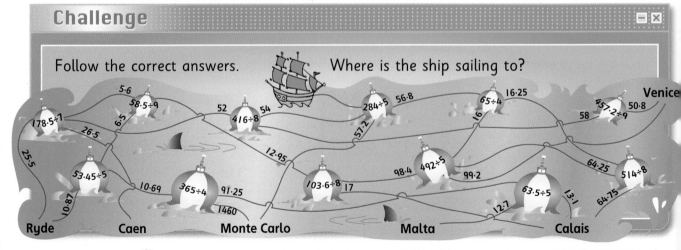

5·6
58·5÷9
52
416÷8
54
284÷5
56·8
65÷4
16·25
457·2÷9
50·8
Venice
178·5÷7
26·5
6·5
57·2
16
58
25·5
53·45÷5
10·69
365÷4
91·25
12·95
103·6÷8 17
98·4 492÷5
99·2
64·25
514÷8
10·87
1460
12·7
63·5÷5
13·1
64·75

Ryde   Caen   Monte Carlo   Malta   Calais

Can you use a written method to divide numbers with up to 2 decimal places by a single-digit number?

A Find each answer. Show your working. Approximate first.

1 143 × 24
2 127 × 36
3 264 × 31
4 341 × 28
5 436 × 46
6 293 × 49

B Write a 'real life' word problem for each calculation. Work out each answer.

7 153 × 22
8 222 × 17
9 152 × 36
10 286 × 34

C Answer these and check each answer. Approximate first.

11 792 ÷ 24
12 910 ÷ 26
13 731 ÷ 43
14 936 ÷ 36
15 798 ÷ 21
16 966 ÷ 23

D Write a 'real life' word problem for each calculation. Work out each answer.

17 952 ÷ 28
18 702 ÷ 18
19 756 ÷ 28
20 928 ÷ 32

E Solve these problems.

21 Boxes contain 345 pins. How many pins in 34 boxes?
22 Flight tickets cost £524 each. What is the cost of 23 tickets?
23 In a car rally, each car travels 946 km. What is the total distance travelled by 26 cars?
24 A school pays £945 for 35 footballs. What is the cost of each football?
25 In 24 weeks a caretaker works for 888 hours. If he works the same number of hours each week, how many hours does he work in 4 weeks?
26 A train travels between 2 towns. After 17 return journeys the train has travelled 884 miles. What is the distance between the towns?
27 Ron Number packs 438 boxes each with 48 drawing pins. He should have packed the pins in boxes of 36. How many boxes will he need to pack all of the pins with 36 in each box?

Challenge
─ ✕

Play with a partner. Use number cards 1 to 9 and a large copy of this grid. In turn, deal 5 cards onto the grid. Work out the answer. Add together the digits in your answer. The player whose answer has the higher digit total scores a point.
The first with 6 points wins the game.
For example, answer 8028, digit total = 18.

×

Can you use a written method for long multiplication and long division?

55

Open sesame!

You need: ● a partner ● a calculator ● 2 sets of 30 counters

How to play

Take turns to choose a question from the bank. Place a counter next to the question. Answer it. Find the answer on one of the safe doors and cover it with another counter.

Score as shown in the Scoring Rules.

The winner is the player with the most points when all the doors are covered so the safes are open!

Scoring Rules

Complete a row of 3 or a column of 3

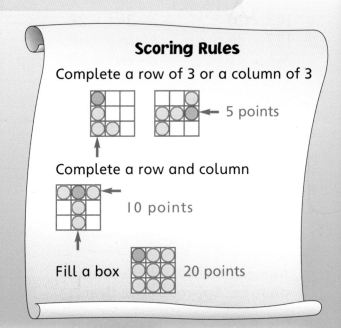

← 5 points

Complete a row and column

10 points

Fill a box   20 points

⁻24	0·069	4056
39	3969	13·2
0·009	⁻25	532

3·2	45	4182
⁻28	4752	462
174	16	10·75

325	693·1	⁻27
4553	15·6	3151
99	4004	12·625

QUESTION BANK

16·5 × 6	64 ÷ 20	154 × 26	607·2 ÷ 46	6·9 ÷ 100	720 ÷ 45
189 × 21	137 × 23	78 ÷ 5	3·48 × 50	38 × 14	9 ÷ 1000
(17 + 8) × 13	⁻42 + 17	264 × 18	338 × 12	⁻18 − 6	(4 × 8) + 7
123 × 34	6·931 × 100	12 − 40	101 ÷ 8	43 ÷ 4	157 × 29
4·62 × 100	⁻11 − 16	315 ÷ 7			

A Solve these problems. Check your answers.

1 If diaries cost £4·15 and biros cost 85p, how many diaries and biros can be bought for exactly £20?

2 Two consecutive numbers have a sum of 45 and a product of 506. What are the 2 numbers?

3 Rides on a helicopter cost £44 for adults and £18 for children. If the cost for a group of people is £186, how many adults and how many children are in the group?

4 Three consecutive numbers have a sum of 240. What are the 3 numbers?

5 Colwill Junior School raised £72·90 by selling programmes for the summer fair. How many programmes were sold if each programme cost 45p?

COLWILL PROGRAMME
45p

Sam is paid £5·30 per hour. He works 40 hours each week. If he works more than 40 hours he is then paid £7·95 per hour. How much does he earn in a week when he works for:

6 42 hours   7 50 hours

8 63 hours?

9 A factory packs sweets with 80 in a jar. Copy and complete this table for the factory.

sweets made	10 000	25 000	120 000	250 000	1 000 000
jars needed					

10 A hotel buys bars of soap for 33p. How many bars can be bought for £100?

11 Matchsticks are 48 mm in length. How many matchsticks can be made from a 1 m stick?

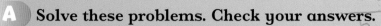

12 A famous football pitch is being replaced. Plots of grass with an area of 1 m² are sold for £15 each. The pitch measures 110 m by 75 m. How many 1 m² plots can be sold?

13 If half the plots of grass above are sold, how much money is raised?

Challenge

From these clues, work out the number represented by each coloured dot.
Each number has 2 digits.

● × ● × ● = 1728   ● × ● = 903   ● × ● = 3510   ● × ● × ● = 5832

● × ● = 516   39% of ● = 30·42   1176 ÷ ● = ●   (● × ●) ÷ ● = 63

Is this statement true? ● × ● > ● × ●

Exchange rates   £1 =   USA 1·75 dollars ($)   Switzerland 2·2 francs (SF)
South Africa 11·1 rand (R)   Malta 0·61 lire (L)   France 1·42 euros (€)

A **Copy and complete this table to show how much currency you would receive.**

Value in:	£10	£40	£100	£350	£1000
1 US dollars ($)	17·50				
2 Swiss francs (SF)					
3 South African rand (R)					
4 Maltese lire (L)		24·4			
5 Euros (€)					

B **Rewrite each menu giving the costs in pounds to the nearest 1p.**

6

American Pie Restaurant

Soup $2
Chicken Salad.. $5
Chocolate Pie .. $3
Coffee.......... $1·50

7

Zurich Zone

Prawn
  Cocktail.... 10SF
Sausages 15SF
Fruit Salad 7SF
Coffee........... 4SF

8

The **Cape** *Café*

Soup 35R
Fish Dish 65R
Dessert 40R
Coffee 25R

9

The Med

Salad 2L
Lasagne ...... 4·5L
Trifle .... 2·5L
Lemonade .. 0·8L

10

L'Auberge

Hors d'oeuvre ..€3
Fruits
  de mer .... €12·5
Ice-cream €4
Coffee .... €2·5

Challenge ▭☒

Work out the perimeter of each garden. Find the cost of building a fence around each perimeter in the currency of the country and also the cost in pounds.

a The American Garden

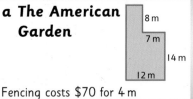
8 m
7 m
14 m
12 m

Fencing costs $70 for 4 m

b The Swiss Garden

6 m   6 m
7 m
7 m
3 m   15 m

Fencing costs 65SF for 3 m

c The Maltese Garden

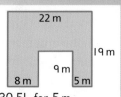
22 m
19 m
9 m
8 m   5 m

Fencing costs 30·5L for 5 m

d Draw a French garden and write questions about it for a partner.

A   Solve these problems.

1   At a conference there is space in each room for 17 people. If 15 rooms are full and there are 8 people in the 16th room, how many people are at the conference?

2   Boxes contain the same number of matches. There are 1440 matches in 30 boxes. How many matches are there in 25 boxes?

3   The sum of 3 numbers is 108. The first number is $\frac{1}{2}$ of 90 and the second number is half of the third number. What are the 3 numbers?

4   Ella thinks of a number, subtracts 9·4 and multiplies it by 12. Her answer is 42. What is the number she thought of?

5   Ian and Jim have been given £25 to spend at the fair. Ian has 2 rides on the Dodgems, 1 on the Helter Skelter and a candy floss. Jim has 2 rides on the

Dodgems	£1·50
Waltzer	£2·25
Helter Skelter	£1·25
Candy floss	£1·80

Waltzer, 1 on the Dodgems and a candy floss. How much money have they left?

6   The sum of 3 numbers is 400. The first number is $\frac{3}{8}$ of 992. The second number is 3 times the third number. What is the product of the second and third numbers?

7   In a junior school there are 90 children in year 3 and year 5, 85 in year 4 and 84 in year 6. Half of the children in year 3 and year 6 come to school by bus. $\frac{4}{5}$ of the children in year 5 and $\frac{3}{5}$ of the children in year 4 do not travel by bus. How many children in the school travel by bus?

8   Doug Earth has visited the garden centre. He buys a crab apple tree, a rose plant and 8 geraniums. He spends £60·45. If the tree cost £34·50 and the rose cost £8·75, what is the cost of 1 geranium?

Challenge   – x

Each letter represents a number less than 40. Use the clues to work out the value of each letter.

u − e = 6	a + s = 24	u + u + e = 27	o − r = 3
a + c = 10	c × u = 22	t ÷ o = 2·5	a × e = 40
y × r = 27	r ÷ y = 3	b × c = 72	o + e + y = 20
b − t = 6	s − a = 8	o + t = 42	b ÷ r = 4

Now crack this code: 3 12 11 ~ 8 9 5 ~ 8 ~ 16 30 8 9.

Can you solve 'story' problems about numbers in 'real life' and puzzles?

59

A **Answer these.**

1 $\frac{1}{8}$ of £24   5 $\frac{1}{5}$ of £75

2 $\frac{1}{6}$ of £18   6 $\frac{1}{10}$ of £830

3 $\frac{1}{3}$ of £60   7 $\frac{1}{9}$ of £108

4 $\frac{1}{8}$ of £64   8 $\frac{1}{4}$ of £600

B **Write as decimal fractions.**

9 $\frac{3}{10}$ 11 $\frac{9}{10}$ 13 $\frac{1}{4}$ 15 $\frac{7}{10}$

10 $\frac{1}{2}$ 12 $\frac{2}{5}$ 14 $\frac{4}{5}$ 16 $\frac{3}{4}$

C **Write the sign < or > to make each correct.**

17 $\frac{3}{5}$ $\frac{4}{10}$ 19 $\frac{9}{10}$ $\frac{4}{5}$ 21 $\frac{1}{2}$ $\frac{3}{5}$

18 $\frac{7}{10}$ $\frac{3}{5}$ 20 $\frac{1}{2}$ $\frac{2}{5}$ 22 $\frac{3}{10}$ $\frac{3}{5}$

D **For each write an equivalent decimal fraction. Use a calculator.**

23 $\frac{1}{8}$ 25 $\frac{3}{16}$ 27 $\frac{1}{20}$ 29 $\frac{11}{20}$

24 $\frac{3}{8}$ 26 $\frac{9}{20}$ 28 $\frac{5}{8}$ 30 $\frac{13}{16}$

E **Write as decimal fractions to 2 places of decimals.**

31 $\frac{1}{7}$ 34 $\frac{1}{11}$

32 $\frac{2}{7}$ 35 $\frac{6}{7}$

33 $\frac{5}{6}$ 36 $\frac{2}{3}$ 37 $\frac{1}{13}$

31 0·14

F **Write each set in ascending order.**

38 $\frac{1}{5}$ $\frac{2}{7}$ $\frac{1}{4}$ $\frac{2}{5}$

39 $\frac{5}{6}$ $\frac{4}{7}$ $\frac{3}{8}$ $\frac{3}{4}$

40 $\frac{4}{5}$ $\frac{6}{7}$ $\frac{7}{8}$ $\frac{8}{9}$

41 $\frac{2}{3}$ $\frac{3}{5}$ $\frac{5}{8}$ $\frac{3}{7}$ 42 $\frac{7}{10}$ $\frac{4}{7}$ $\frac{2}{3}$ $\frac{5}{6}$ 43 $\frac{3}{11}$ $\frac{4}{13}$ $\frac{3}{10}$ $\frac{5}{9}$

38 $\frac{1}{5}$ $\frac{1}{4}$ $\frac{2}{7}$ $\frac{2}{5}$

G **Write 4 equivalent fractions.**

44 $\frac{2}{3}$ 46 $\frac{3}{4}$ 48 $\frac{2}{7}$

45 $\frac{3}{5}$ 47 $\frac{3}{10}$ 49 $\frac{3}{8}$

44 $\frac{4}{6}$ $\frac{6}{9}$ $\frac{10}{15}$ $\frac{20}{30}$

Challenge ▢✕

Find circles that have the same values as the fractions below. Work out the coded message.

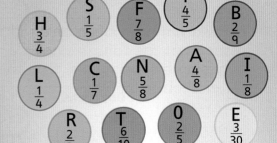

H $\frac{3}{4}$ S $\frac{1}{5}$ F $\frac{7}{8}$ Y $\frac{4}{5}$ B $\frac{2}{9}$

L $\frac{1}{4}$ C $\frac{1}{7}$ N $\frac{5}{8}$ A $\frac{4}{8}$ I $\frac{1}{8}$

R $\frac{2}{3}$ T $\frac{6}{10}$ O $\frac{2}{5}$ E $\frac{3}{30}$

$\frac{1}{2}$ | $\frac{14}{16}$ $\frac{4}{6}$ $\frac{1}{2}$ $\frac{3}{21}$ $\frac{3}{5}$ $\frac{2}{16}$ $\frac{6}{15}$ $\frac{10}{16}$

$\frac{6}{60}$ $\frac{8}{16}$ $\frac{6}{9}$ $\frac{2}{8}$ $\frac{8}{10}$ | $\frac{3}{24}$ $\frac{2}{10}$ | $\frac{4}{18}$ $\frac{1}{10}$ $\frac{3}{5}$ $\frac{12}{20}$ $\frac{9}{90}$ $\frac{4}{6}$

$\frac{3}{5}$ $\frac{75}{100}$ $\frac{50}{100}$ $\frac{20}{32}$ | $\frac{9}{18}$ | $\frac{4}{16}$ $\frac{10}{80}$ $\frac{60}{100}$ $\frac{30}{50}$ $\frac{25}{100}$ $\frac{1}{10}$

$\frac{10}{40}$ $\frac{500}{1000}$ $\frac{30}{50}$ $\frac{1}{10}$

Create a coded message for a partner using a different set of equivalent fractions.

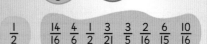

Can you change a fraction to an equivalent fraction by multiplying or dividing the numerator and denominator by the same number?

A Does a fraction become larger, smaller or stay the same size if you:

1 double the denominator
2 treble the numerator
3 double both the denominator and numerator
4 multiply both the numerator and denominator by 100?

B Copy and complete this table. Write equivalent fractions with the denominator shown.

	Fractions		New denominator	Equivalent fractions
5	$\frac{1}{2}$	$\frac{1}{3}$	6	$\frac{3}{6}$, $\frac{2}{6}$
6	$\frac{1}{4}$	$\frac{1}{3}$	12	
7	$\frac{3}{5}$	$\frac{1}{2}$	10	
8	$\frac{4}{5}$	$\frac{1}{3}$	15	
9	$\frac{3}{10}$	$\frac{3}{4}$	20	
10	$\frac{1}{6}$	$\frac{3}{4}$	12	
11	$\frac{5}{6}$	$\frac{2}{9}$	18	

C Give equivalent fractions so that the fractions in each pair have a common denominator.

12 $\frac{1}{2}$ $\frac{2}{3}$ 15 $\frac{1}{6}$ $\frac{3}{4}$ 12 $\frac{3}{6}$ $\frac{4}{6}$

13 $\frac{3}{4}$ $\frac{1}{3}$ 16 $\frac{2}{5}$ $\frac{2}{3}$

14 $\frac{3}{5}$ $\frac{1}{4}$ 17 $\frac{1}{6}$ $\frac{3}{8}$ 18 $\frac{2}{9}$ $\frac{4}{5}$

D Copy the red number line below onto squared paper. Draw arrows to show the position of each fraction.

0 ——————————————— 1

$\frac{1}{2}$

19 $\frac{1}{2}$ 22 $\frac{1}{6}$ 25 $\frac{5}{6}$
20 $\frac{1}{4}$ 23 $\frac{3}{4}$ 26 $\frac{3}{8}$
21 $\frac{1}{3}$ 24 $\frac{2}{3}$ 27 $\frac{7}{12}$

Challenge ▬ ☒

Play with a partner. Use number cards 1 to 9 and a large copy of this grid.

□ / □ of £ ▢ ▢

Take turns. Shuffle the cards.
Place the first 2 cards on the yellow sections of the grid to make a fraction with the denominator larger than the numerator.
Place the next 2 cards after the £ sign. Work out the grid value to the nearest 1p.
The player with the higher amount scores a point.
The first to 10 points wins.
Try the game with larger card numbers and 3 sections after the £ sign.

Can you use a fraction as an operator to find fractions of numbers or quantities?

61

A Find how many: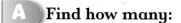

1 quarters in 6
2 fifths in 10
3 eighths in 7
4 sixths in $5\frac{1}{2}$
5 tenths in $7\frac{1}{5}$
6 twelfths in 8.

B Write as improper fractions.

7 $4\frac{1}{4}$ 9 $3\frac{2}{5}$ 11 $5\frac{3}{8}$ 13 $2\frac{9}{10}$
8 $5\frac{1}{5}$ 10 $6\frac{2}{3}$ 12 $7\frac{3}{4}$ 14 $4\frac{5}{6}$

C Write as mixed numbers.

15 $\frac{16}{3}$ 17 $\frac{19}{5}$ 19 $\frac{17}{9}$ 21 $\frac{30}{7}$
16 $\frac{15}{4}$ 18 $\frac{21}{6}$ 20 $\frac{15}{6}$ 22 $\frac{41}{5}$

D Copy and complete this table.

	Percentage	Fraction	Decimal Fraction
23	10%	$\frac{1}{10}$	0·1
24	50%		
25	25%		
26	47%		
27	93%		
28	36%		

E Calculate each exact answer. Estimate first.

29 A house was bought for £90 000. It is now worth $1\frac{2}{3}$ times that amount. How much is the house worth?
30 How much is 70% of £250?
31 In a delivery of 375 apples, 12% are bad. How many are not bad?
32 How far is 35% of 400 km?
33 In a gym club, 15 members are boys and 70% are girls. How many girls are members?
34 How much is 12·5% of £4200?
35 How much is $2\frac{1}{2}$% of £620?
36 To the nearest whole number, what percentage is 31 out of 70?

Challenge ─ □ ✕

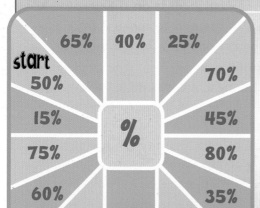

65% 90% 25%
start
50%   70%
15%   **%**   45%
75%   80%
60%   35%
85% 20% 55%

Play with a partner. Use a dice, number cards 0 to 9, a counter and a large copy of the grid below. Shuffle the cards. Take turns to deal 2 cards on the two empty spaces of the grid to form a 3-digit multiple of 10. Roll the dice. Move the counter that number around the track to give a percentage. Work out this percentage of your 3-digit number. The higher answer scores a point. The first to 10 points wins the game.

		0

Can you find percentages of small whole number quantities?

You need: 2 sets of number cards 1 to 9 • a calculator

Shuffle both sets of cards together. Deal cards from the top of the pack onto the grid. Work out the value of each calculation to the nearest whole number. Add your 3 answers together to find your total pinball score.
What is the highest total score you can achieve after 10 turns?

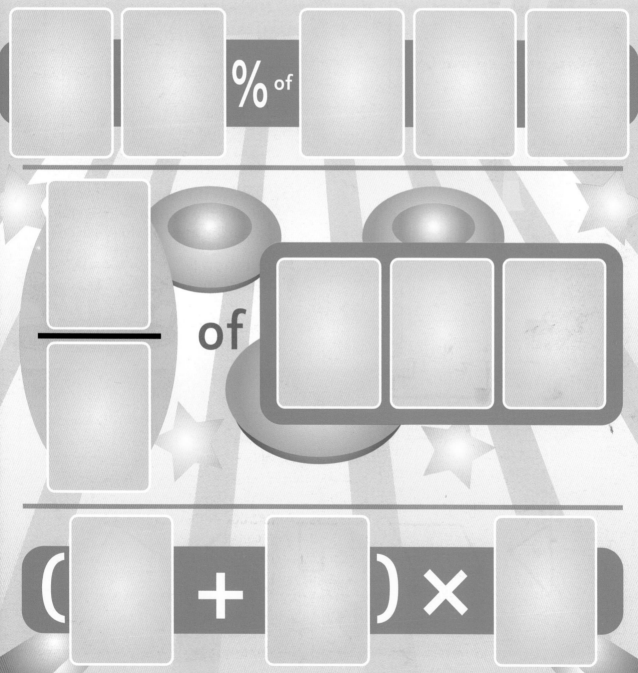

A Copy each shape and the mirror line onto squared paper. Draw the reflection of each shape. Use a mirror to check each reflection.

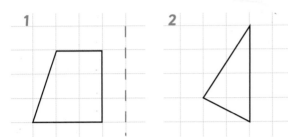

1

2

B Reflect each pattern in the 2 axes of symmetry.

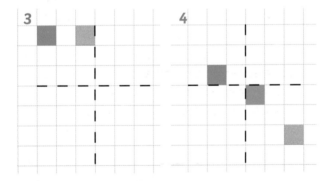

3

4

C Copy each diagram onto squared paper. Show the position of each shape after a rotation of 90° anti-clockwise about the origin.

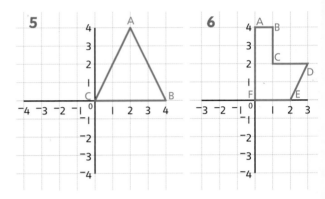

5

6

D Rotate the shapes above 180° about the origin. Write the new co-ordinates of the vertices.

7 question 5
8 question 6

Challenge ▢ ✕

Copy each shape onto squared paper.
Rotate each shape 90° anti-clockwise about point Z.
Draw the shape in its new position.

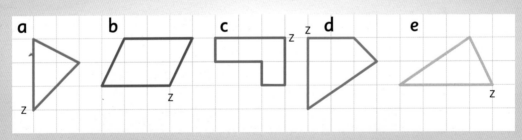

a **b** **c** **d** **e**

Can you recognize where a shape will be after a rotation of 90 degrees or 180 degrees about a vertex?

A Copy each shape onto squared paper. Draw the reflection of each shape in the mirror line.

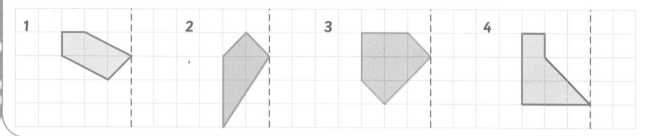

1　　　　　　2　　　　　　3　　　　　　4

B Find the coordinates of the reflected point when each point is reflected in the y axis.

C Find the coordinates of the reflected point when each point is reflected in the x axis.

5　(⁻4,2)　　　7　(2,8)　　　9　(⁻1,0)
6　(⁻6,3)　　　8　(⁻3,⁻6)　　10　(⁻4,⁻7)

11　(3,6)　　　13　(5,⁻7)　　　15　(⁻4,⁻7)
12　(2,⁻1)　　14　(⁻6,2)　　　16　(0,3)

D These shapes have been reflected in both the x and y axes. Give the coordinates of the vertices of each reflected shape.

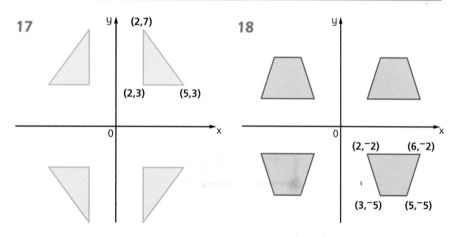

17

18

Challenge

a Study the coordinates of the 4 shapes in question 17. Write about any patterns you can find. Repeat for the 4 sets of coordinates in question 18.

b Draw a quadrilateral in the first quadrant on a grid. Reflect the quadrilateral in both the x and y axes. Write down the coordinates of the vertices of all 4 quadrilaterals. Can you find any patterns?

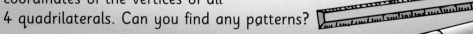

Can you recognize where a shape will be after reflection in a line touching the shape at a point?

65

A Copy each shape on a grid. Draw the reflection of each shape in the mirror line.

1   2   3   4

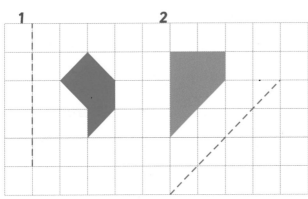

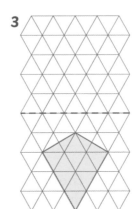

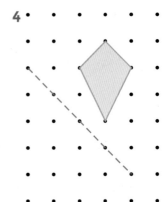

B Describe the reflection or rotation that would move shape Z to each different position.

5 Y   6 X   7 W

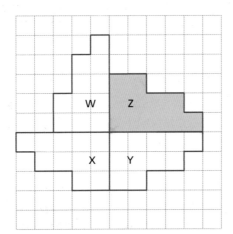

C Copy this shape and the mirror lines onto squared paper.

8 Reflect the shape in the two mirror lines.

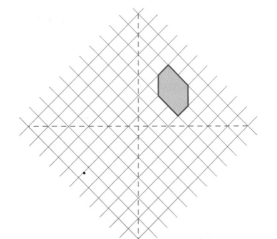

Challenge

Using different grids like the ones on this page, draw shapes for a partner to reflect in one or two mirror lines.

Can you recognize where a shape will be after reflection in 2 mirror lines at right angles?

Review 3

A Write the value of the red digit.

1 4·77   3 1·43   5 2·51
2 3·69   4 8·69   6 4·86

B Round to the nearest tenth.

7 2·91   9 4·07   11 3·95
8 3·87   10 6·85

C Round to the nearest hundredth.

12 3·281   14 7·046   16 6·831
13 5·968   15 3·825

D Answer these. Give each quotient as a fraction.

17 46 ÷ 7   20 81 ÷ 2   22 101 ÷ 5
18 59 ÷ 10   21 73 ÷ 4   23 97 ÷ 8
19 38 ÷ 5

E Answer these.

24 392 ÷ 5
25 413 ÷ 6   30 263 × 32
26 218 ÷ 9   31 348 × 28
27 716 ÷ 8   32 427 × 26
28 333 ÷ 6   33 196 × 36
29 126 × 37   34 283 × 42

F Solve these problems.

35 Roses cost 55p each. How many roses can be bought for £50?
36 Two consecutive numbers have a sum of 51 and a product of 650. What are the numbers?
37 Tins contain the same number of pins. There are 2000 pins in 25 tins. How many pins are there in 10 tins?

G Write as a decimal fraction to 2 places of decimals. Use a calculator.

38 $\frac{1}{7}$ 40 $\frac{3}{11}$ 42 $\frac{2}{3}$
39 $\frac{5}{6}$ 41 $\frac{7}{9}$ 43 $\frac{8}{13}$

H Write as mixed numbers.

44 $\frac{17}{4}$ 47 $\frac{25}{7}$ 49 $\frac{71}{9}$
45 $\frac{16}{9}$ 48 $\frac{34}{8}$ 50 $\frac{50}{6}$
46 $\frac{13}{3}$

I Answer these.

51 30% of £350   55 15% of £960
52 70% of £150   56 85% of £990
53 90% of £560   57 55% of £750
54 35% of £420

J Copy each shape onto squared paper. Rotate each shape 180° about the red dot. Draw the shape in its new position.

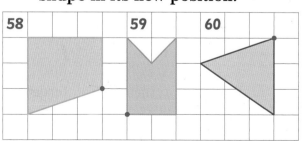

58   59   60

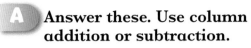

A Answer these. Use column addition or subtraction.

1 2438 + 1463
2 1764 + 5678
3 4235 − 1628
4 5168 − 3759
5 9301 − 2471
6 3867 + 8427
7 3956 + 9627
8 5063 − 2747

B Answer these. Use a column method.

9   12·63 − 1·42
10 12·96 − 7·89
11 8·37 − 4·68
12 16·36 + 14·87
13 11·95 + 6·07
14 7·54 − 2·68
15 16·42 − 11·96
16 20·03 − 17·64

C Find two decimal numbers with these differences.

17 4·9
18 6·1
19 4·3
20 6·4
21 11·9
22 20·5

17 11·7 and 6·8

D Work out the missing number.

23
  24·26
− ⬛⬤·⬛⬤
  11·74

24
  36·51
− ⬛✳·⬛⬛
  24·93

25
  28·07
− ⬤▲·▲⬛
  16·39

26
  30·45
− ⬛⬤·⬤⬛
  19·99

23 12·52

E Answer these. Show your working or write Ⓗ if you do them in your head.

27
  301·2
− 199·8
_____

28
  632·7
+ 165·9
_____

29
  116·25
− 17·99
_____

30
  4317·85
+ 682·15
_____

Challenge   ⊟⊠

Play with a partner. Each use a set of number cards 0 to 9, a large copy of this grid, and a set of six red numbers. Place the cards on the grid to get as close as you can to the target number. Work out the difference between your numbers and the target number. Repeat for each target. Find the sum of all six differences. The player with the lower total for all six differences wins.

a
1 2 3 4 5 6
target 40·6

b
6 7 4 3 2 1
target 50·5

c
4 5 7 3 8 9
target 37·4

d
3 8 7 2 4 6
target 33·5

e
3 4 6 5 7 9
target 11·5

f
5 9 2 3 8 7
target 56·3

 Can you use a written method for column addition and subtraction of numbers involving decimals?

A Answer these, showing your working. Estimate first.

1 Jake has saved £46·23. He buys a shirt for £17·68. How much money has he left?

2 A length of string is 50 m. After 37·59 m is cut off, how much string is left?

3 Fatima buys 4 books costing £5·95, £6·25, £12·98 and £3·85. Nadine buys 3 books costing £11·65, £10·99 and £2·58. How much more does Fatima spend than Nadine?

4 If Fatima started out with £30, how much money has she left?

5 A sack of flour weighed 50 kg. A chef took 12·75 kg, then 11·64 kg. What does the sack weigh now?

6 John thinks of a number, he adds 12·4 and then subtracts 5·7. His answer is 15·2. What was the number he thought of?

7 Ivor Pressy has 3 £20 gift vouchers and 4 £5 vouchers for a store. He buys a saucepan for £17·90, a game for £22·65 and a vase for £12·85. How much has he left to spend?

8 How much would Ivor have left to spend if the shop had reduced all its prices by 20% in a sale?

B Copy and complete this table for each pair of numbers A and B.

	A	B	A + B	A − B
9	16	2	18	14
10	19			4
11			22	8
12	4·7		18·9	
13		13·5		6·6
14	7	⁻6		
15	3			⁻1
16		4		⁻3
17	8·4			⁻1·6

Challenge

T 32·92 − 1·85   S 219·87 + 116·38
E 423·8 − 62·9   I 49·29 + 112·16
B 37·26 − 18·57   I 45·76 − 26·8
A 19·81 − 6·95   G 39·72 − 19·65
O 11·64 + 19·83   T 112·81 − 64·9
R 117·93 − 84·26   O 123·45 − 54·98

Answer each question. Write the answers in order, smallest first. Write the letters that go with each answer in the same order. This will tell you what is in the crate. Make up a similar code using decimal numbers. Ask your partner to work it out.

DO NOT OPEN

DANGEROUS ANIMAL!

Can you use appropriate operations to solve word problems involving numbers and quantities?

69

A In magic squares the sum of the numbers in any line, horizontal, vertical and diagonal is the same. Copy and complete these magic squares.

1

2·6		
1·6		2·4
1·8		

2

		3·96
2·64	5·94	1·32

3

		17·6	7·92
	10·56	9·68	
	14·08		8·8
15·84	6·16		18·48

B Answer each question. Check by rounding or by using the inverse operation.

4 (16·24 + 8·95) − (36·3 − 21·4)
5 (34·8 − 7·3) + (24·5 − 12·9)
6 (34·21 − 16·83) + (14·49 − 6·87)
7 (21·48 + 12·69) − (16·54 + 2·68)
8 (53·19 + 12·72) − (6·37 + 18·54)
9 (34·63 − 16·47) + (8·94 + 16·66)

C Without using a calculator choose which answer is correct.

10 16·7 + 149·36 **316·06** **216·06** **166·0**

11 94·85 × 7 **663·36** **663·95** **66·395**

12 26·85 × 4 **107·45** **97·45** **107·4**

13 996·2 − 389·7 **606·5** **613·5** **506·5**

14 7·956 ÷ 9 **8·84** **63·604** **0·884**

15 3·655 × 6 **12·93** **219·3** **21·93**

16 46·85 ÷ 0·5 **9·37** **93·7** **93·4**

Challenge ▬ ✕

Play with a partner. Use 2 sets of 14 counters, a dice and a large copy of this grid. Take turns to roll

	odd	even	odd	even	
odd	even	odd	even	odd	even
	odd	even	odd	even	
		odd	even		
even	odd	even	odd	even	odd
	even	odd	even	odd	

the dice and move around the track to collect odd or even numbers.
Make up some rules to decide how you will choose the winner of the game.

ODD or EVEN?

- sum of an odd number of odd numbers is
- product of 2 even numbers is
- sum of 2 or more even numbers is
- sum of odd and even number is
- product of 2 odd numbers is
- difference between 2 even numbers is
- difference between even and odd number is
- difference between odd and even number is
- product of odd and even number is
- sum of an even number of odd numbers is
- sum of even and odd number is
- difference between 2 odd numbers is

Can you use knowledge of sums, differences or products of odd and even numbers?

A Work out the area of each shape in square centimetres.

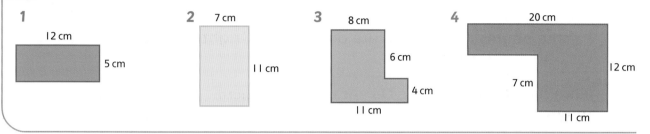

1
12 cm
5 cm

2
7 cm
11 cm

3
8 cm
6 cm
4 cm
11 cm

4
20 cm
12 cm
7 cm
11 cm

B Estimate the size of each angle. Say whether it is acute or obtuse.

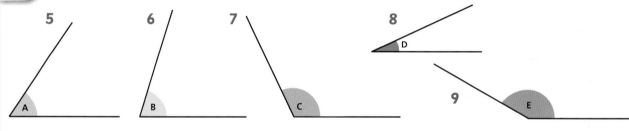

5 A

6 B

7 C

8 D

9 E

10 Measure each angle above to the nearest 1°. Copy and complete this table.

Angle	A	B	C	D	E
To nearest 1°					

C Draw each angle as accurately as you can.

11 45°	13 62°	15 146°
12 25°	14 111°	16 174°

D Give the size of each angle without measuring.

17 67°

18 34°

19 144°

20 42°

Challenge

Draw any quadrilateral on a piece of paper. Mark the angles A, B, C and D. Carefully cut out the quadrilateral. Tear off the angles. Place them together. What do you find? Try this with four different quadrilaterals.

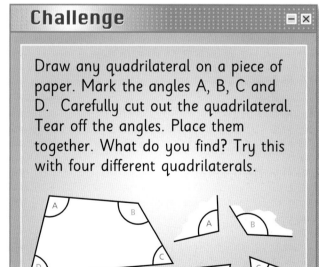

Can you use a protractor to measure and draw acute and obtuse angles to the nearest degree?

A Draw a quadrilateral with these properties.

1 2 obtuse angles
2 3 acute angles
3 3 obtuse angles
4 2 acute angles and 1 right angle

B Find the missing angles. Do not use a protractor.

5
60° 40°

7
70° 120°

9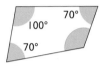
45°

11 70° 100° 70°

6
110° 35°

8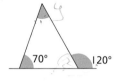
120° 70° 95°

10 75° 35°

C Say whether or not each is the net of a closed cube.

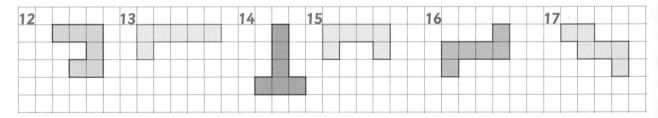

12 13 14 15 16 17

Challenge

Work out the size of each angle.
Do not use a protractor.
Use your information to crack
this secret angle code.

41° a   y   b 152°   u
55° 81°
e s   n
50° 83° c   105° t   66° o

a = 40°

47° 40° 66°   40°   47° 98° 75° 56°   44° 40° 44° 151°

44° 56°   24° 44° 75° 98° 153° 56°?

Can you visualize 3D shapes from 2D drawings and identify different nets for a closed cube?

A Look at this diagram.

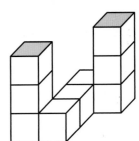

1 Find the smallest number of cubes you would need to form a bridge from one orange platform to the other.
2 Explain how you worked out your answer.

B Use cm-squared paper.

3 Draw a net for a square-based pyramid.

C Work out the perimeter and area of each shape.

4 perimeter 34 m
area 52 m²

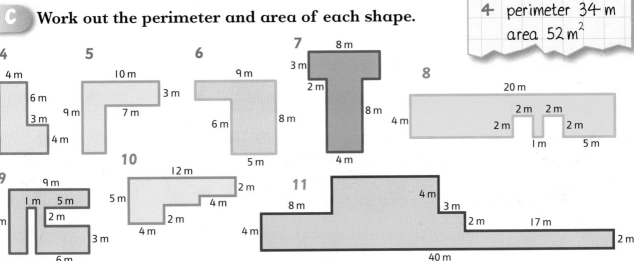

4
4 m
6 m
3 m
9 m
4 m

5
10 m
3 m
7 m
9 m

6
9 m
6 m
8 m
5 m

7
8 m
3 m
2 m
8 m
4 m

8
20 m
2 m 2 m
2 m 2 m
4 m
1 m 5 m

9
9 m
1 m 5 m
2 m
7 m
3 m
6 m

10
12 m
2 m
5 m 4 m
2 m
4 m

11
4 m
8 m 3 m
4 m 2 m 17 m
40 m 2 m

Challenge

Junior Giles has been told by his father that he can have an area of land of 36 m² to grow some vegetables. His plot of land must be rectangular, with each side measuring a whole number of metres. Draw sketches to show the rectangle with its measurements that:

a has the shortest perimeter
b has the longest perimeter
c has a perimeter of 30 m
d has a perimeter of 40 m.

e Sketch one other rectangular shape that Junior Giles could choose.

Can you calculate the perimeter and area of simple shapes that can be split into rectangles?

73

You need:

● a partner   ● 2 sets of 10 counters   ● a protractor   ● a calculator

Place a counter on any section of the track.
Both estimate the answer to the challenge in that section.
Check your answers with a calculator or a protractor.
If you have the closer estimate, place a counter on the chequered flag below.
Now both estimate the answer to the challenge in the next section.
The winner is the first to have an unbroken line of 3 counters on the flag.

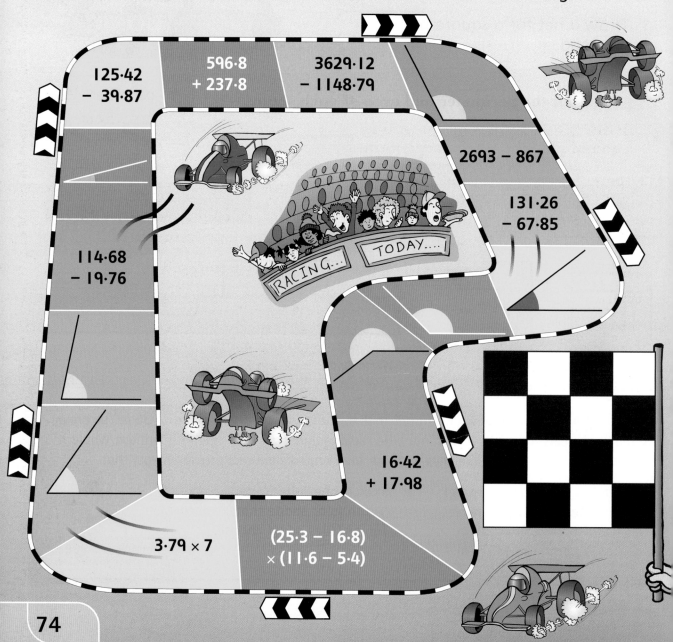

125·42
− 39·87

596·8
+ 237·8

3629·12
− 1148·79

2693 − 867

131·26
− 67·85

114·68
− 19·76

16·42
+ 17·98

3·79 × 7

(25·3 − 16·8)
× (11·6 − 5·4)

RACING... TODAY....

A Write in metres.

1 361 cm
2 438 cm
3 409 cm
4 1260 cm

B Write in millilitres.

5 $\frac{1}{2}$ l   6 $\frac{3}{4}$ l   7 $2\frac{1}{10}$ l   8 3·6 l

C Write in grams.

9   $\frac{1}{2}$ kg
10 1·2 kg   11 3·8 kg

D Give two examples of something you might measure in each unit.

12 pints
13 miles
14 ounces
15 kilograms
16 centilitres
17 millimetres
18 tonnes
19 metres
20 gallons
21 inches

E Solve these problems.

22 Phil Mycup has 2 kettles. The small one holds 740 ml of water and the larger one holds $3\frac{1}{4}$ times as much. How much water does the second kettle hold?

23 Mrs Cotton is knitting a scarf that will be 1m long. On 3 days she has knitted $42\frac{1}{2}$ cm, 320 mm and 0·2 m. What length of scarf has still to be knitted?

24 3 parcels weigh 1·85 kg, 5·2 kg and 850 g. What is the total mass of the 3 parcels?

25 Which is the better value, 750 g of potatoes for 84p or a 5 kg bag for £5·70?

26 Which is the better value, 50 cm of tape costing 11p or a 75 m roll of the tape costing £18?

Challenge

Play with a partner. Use 2 counters, a dice, and a score sheet. Roll the dice and take turns to move around the track. Keep your score in grams (for example, 1·2 kg = 1200 grams). The first to collect a total of 10 000 grams wins the game.

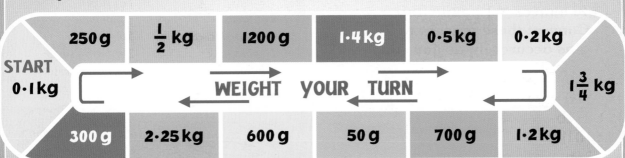

| 250 g | $\frac{1}{2}$ kg | 1200 g | 1·4 kg | 0·5 kg | 0·2 kg |

START
0·1 kg

WEIGHT YOUR TURN

$1\frac{3}{4}$ kg

| 300 g | 2·25 kg | 600 g | 50 g | 700 g | 1·2 kg |

Can you convert smaller to larger units of capacity and mass and vice versa?

75

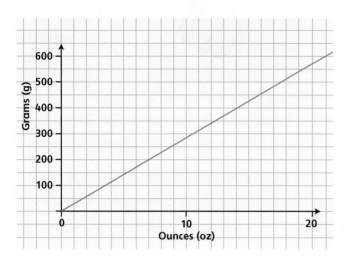

Use the conversion graph.

A Find the approximate mass in grams.

1	12 oz	4	8 oz
2	14 oz	5	16 oz
3	2 oz	6	20 oz

B Find the approximate mass in ounces.

7	300 g	10	500 g
8	275 g	11	250 g
9	50 g	12	525 g

C 16 ounces = 1 pound (lb).
Convert these masses to kg and g as accurately as you can.

13 3 lb
14 5 lb
15 $3\frac{1}{2}$ lb
16 10 lb
17 2 lb
18 100 lb

13 approximately
1 kg 350 g

D Find which colour arrow points to each measurement.

19 the mass of a new-born baby
20 the capacity of a watering can
21 the mass of a bag of sugar
22 the capacity of a milk bottle
23 the mass of a coffee mug
24 the capacity of 12 tea cups

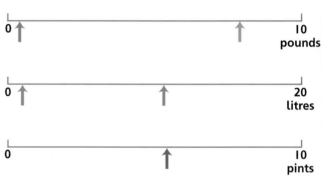

Challenge

Rewrite these recipes using metric units.

Cheese and leek soup
2 oz butter
12 oz leeks
2 onions
2 oz flour
$1\frac{1}{2}$ pints chicken stock
$1\frac{1}{2}$ pints milk
$\frac{1}{2}$ lb cheese
freshly ground pepper
6 oz yoghurt

Currant buns
8 oz self-raising flour
4 oz butter
1 oz sugar
$\frac{1}{4}$ pint milk
5 oz currants
2 oz brown sugar
1 oz mixed peel
$1\frac{1}{2}$ oz glacé cherries

Do you know the approximate equivalence between commonly used imperial units and metric units?

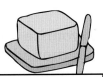

Flour	Butter	Milk	Sugar	Sausages	Cheese
60p per kg	95p per 250 g	64p per litre	96p per kg	8 for £1·28	£5·72 per kg

A Find the cost of these items.

1 $\frac{1}{2}$ kg of cheese
2 4 l of milk
3 12 sausages
4 200 g of butter
5 $3\frac{1}{2}$ kg of sugar
6 750 g of flour
7 $2\frac{1}{2}$ l of milk
8 250 g of sugar
9 3·25 l of milk
10 9 kg of butter

B A recipe for 5 people requires 600 g of flour, 100 g of butter, $\frac{1}{2}$ l of milk and 250 g of sugar. Use this information to answer these.

11 Work out the amount of each ingredient required if the meal needs to be prepared for 8 people.
Find the cost of the ingredients when the meal is prepared for:

12 5 people
13 8 people
14 12 people.

C Use the graph to find each answer.

15 What distance was the journey?
16 How long did the journey take?
17 How far had Clive travelled after $\frac{1}{2}$ hour?
18 At what time did the coach stop for a break?
19 Approximately how far had Clive travelled after $1\frac{1}{4}$ hours?
20 Did Clive travel further between 12:00 and 13:00 or between 14:00 and 15:00?
21 Write 5 more questions about this graph.

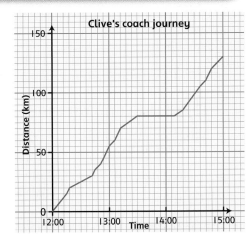

Clive's coach journey

Challenge ☐ ×

Arrange these amounts of money in order of size, smallest first.

25% of £60	40% of £110	5% of £400	$12\frac{1}{2}$% of £80
$17\frac{1}{2}$% of £70	90% of £30	15% of £50	$17\frac{1}{2}$% of £40

Can you solve word problems involving numbers and quantities based on 'real life', money or measures?

77

A Solve these problems.

1 On a farm, for every dog there are 12 sheep. If there are 6 dogs, how many sheep are there?

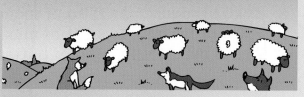

2 There are 24 children in a class. For every boy there are 3 girls. How many boys are in the class?

3 What is the ratio of green grapes to black grapes in this dish?

B Find the ratio measured in grams for these ingredients.

Ingredients for celery soup
Celery 360 g
Potatoes 120 g
Butter 30 g
Cream 150 ml
Milk 200 ml
Chicken stock 600 ml

4 potatoes to celery
5 butter to potatoes
6 butter to celery

Find the ratio measured in ml for these ingredients.

7 milk to chicken stock
8 milk to cream
9 chicken stock to cream

C

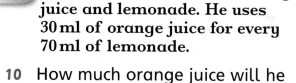

Jason's favourite drink is orange juice and lemonade. He uses 30 ml of orange juice for every 70 ml of lemonade.

10 How much orange juice will he need to make 200 ml of his drink?

11 How much lemonade will he need if he is using 150 ml of orange juice?

12 How much orange juice will he need with 350 ml of lemonade?

13 What quantity of the drink can he make with 105 ml of orange juice?

14 How much orange juice and lemonade will he need to make 550 ml of the drink?

15 Copy and complete this number line for the orange and lemonade mixture.

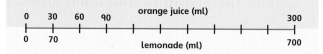

Challenge

Copy these rectangles onto squared paper. Colour the small squares in each shape red or blue in the ratio shown.

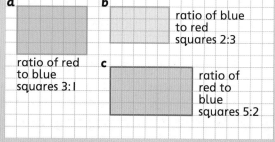

a

b ratio of blue to red squares 2:3

ratio of red to blue squares 3:1

c ratio of red to blue squares 5:2

Can you solve simple problems involving ratio?

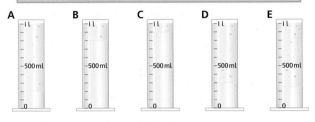

Orange juice and lemonade drinks

A   B   C   D   E

-1 l

-500 ml

0

A Find the proportion of orange juice.

$1\frac{1}{5}$

1   in measure A
2   in measure B   4   in measure D
3   in measure C   5   in measure E

B Find the proportion of lemonade.

6   in measure A   8   in measure D
7   in measure C   9   in measure E

C Solve these problems.

A bag contains 20p and £1 coins. The proportion of 20p coins is $\frac{1}{6}$. There are 36 coins in the bag.

10   How many 20p coins are in the bag?
11   How many £1 coins are in the bag?
12   What is the value of the 20p coins?
13   What is the value of all the money in the bag?
14   If some 50p coins are added to the bag so that the proportion of 50p coins is $\frac{1}{2}$, what will be the value of the 50p coins?
15   In a class the proportion of girls is $\frac{2}{5}$. The proportion of boys wearing red jumpers is $\frac{2}{3}$. If there are 30 children in the class, how many boys are wearing red jumpers?

D Use cm-squared paper.

16   Copy and complete this conversion graph to convert Australian dollars and pounds up to £10.

£1 is worth £2·25 Australian dollars

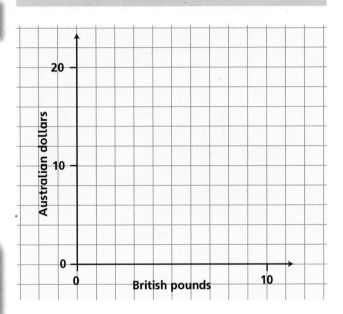

17   Write five questions about your graph for a partner.

Challenge

A South African rand is worth 9p. Draw a conversion graph to help convert rand and pounds for amounts up to £10.
Write five questions about your graph for a partner.

Can you solve a problem using proportion and use a line graph to represent, extract and interpret data?

79

A Use the bar chart to answer these questions.

Daily ice-cream sales for Carlo's van in June, July and August.

1 On how many days did Carlo sell from 31 to 45 ice-creams?
2 On how many days did Carlo sell less than 46 ice-creams?
3 On how many days in June, July and August was Carlo not selling ice-creams?
4 On how many days did he sell more than 60 ice-creams?
5 What do you think the weather was like on these days?
6 What proportion of the days when he sold more than 45 ice-creams did he sell more than 60 ice-creams?

B Estimate the answers to these questions.

7 How many robins did Bill see?
8 How many magpies did Ann see?
9 How many sparrows did Ann see?
10 How many crows did Bill see?
11 Who saw more chaffinches, Ann or Bill?
12 Who saw more greenfinches, Ann or Bill?
13 Approximately how many sparrows were seen altogether in both gardens?
14 Approximately what proportion of greenfinches seen in both gardens were seen by Ann?

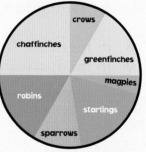

In Bill's garden

Total 60

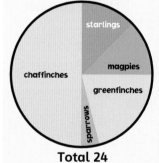

In Ann's garden

Total 24

Challenge ─ □ ✕

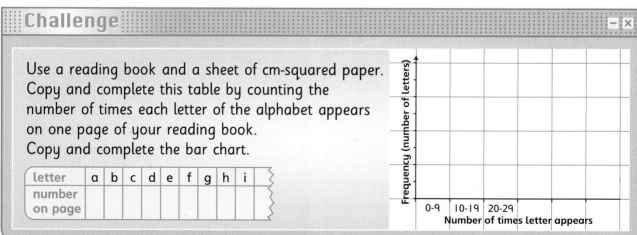

Use a reading book and a sheet of cm-squared paper. Copy and complete this table by counting the number of times each letter of the alphabet appears on one page of your reading book.
Copy and complete the bar chart.

letter	a	b	c	d	e	f	g	h	i
number on page									

Frequency (number of letters)

0-9 | 10-19 | 20-29
Number of times letter appears

Can you extract and interpret data from bar charts using grouped discrete data, and from pie charts?

You need:

- a partner
- 2 sets of 9 counters
- a dice

In turn, roll the dice 10 times and write down your 10 scores.
Rewrite your scores in order, smallest first.
Take turns to roll the dice and count around the track.
When you land on a section, ask, 'What proportion of my scores are ... ?'
Work out the answer.
If your answer is on the cage, cover it with a counter.
The first to place 8 counters on the cage is the winner.

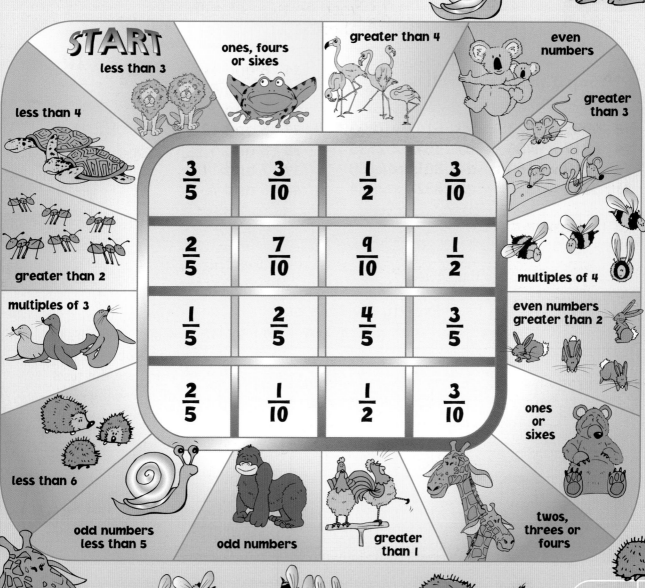

START

less than 3

ones, fours or sixes

greater than 4

even numbers

less than 4

greater than 3

greater than 2

multiples of 4

multiples of 3

even numbers greater than 2

ones or sixes

less than 6

odd numbers less than 5

odd numbers

greater than 1

twos, threes or fours

$\frac{3}{5}$	$\frac{3}{10}$	$\frac{1}{2}$	$\frac{3}{10}$
$\frac{2}{5}$	$\frac{7}{10}$	$\frac{9}{10}$	$\frac{1}{2}$
$\frac{1}{5}$	$\frac{2}{5}$	$\frac{4}{5}$	$\frac{3}{5}$
$\frac{2}{5}$	$\frac{1}{10}$	$\frac{1}{2}$	$\frac{3}{10}$

A   Write the factors of each number.

1 1 2 4 8 16

1 **16**   3 **20**

2 **18**   4 **24**   5 **36**   6 **80**

B   Answer these.

7   7×5 11 7×7 15 6×6

8   9×8 12 6×7 16 4×8

9   6×9 13 8×8 17 9×9

10   8×6 14 8×7

C   Say if the answer will be odd or even.

18   4795×3627 22 6147×7899

19   6217×9406 23 3645×2735

20   3219×4169 24 8612×4169

21   3842×7350 25 8328×7954

D   Find the units digit in the answer.

26   4372×6547 30 8312×4725

27   1279×6436 31 3666×2555

28   4218×1527 32 4901×6999

29   4386×2467 33 4628×8308

E   Write the lowest common multiple and four other common multiples.

34   lcm = 30
     60 90 120 150

34   6 and 10

35   8 and 6

36   5 and 7

37   5 and 12

38   8 and 5

39   7 and 11

40   6 and 7

Challenge

Copy and complete this table.

Number	Exactly divisible by									
	2	3	4	5	6	8	9	10	25	100
6345		✔		✔			✔			
1725										
1233										
4800										
3456										
2952										
3575										

Add eight more 4-digit numbers to your table and complete the tests of divisibility.

Can you apply simple tests of divisibility and find simple common multiples?

A For each set, write four 4-digit numbers.

1 multiples of 2
2 multiples of 5
3 multiples of 3
4 multiples of 10
5 multiples of 9
6 multiples of 4
7 multiples of 6
8 multiples of 7

B Copy and complete this list of all the prime numbers to 100.

9

2, ★, ■, 7, 11, ◖, ◣, ✸, 23,
▲, ⬣, 37, ⬤, 43, ⬤, 53, ⬤,
⬤, 67, ✳, ▲, 79, 83, ⬤, ★

C Give the prime factors.

10 **40**   13 **24**

| 10 | 2 and 5 |

11 **12**   14 **30**

12 **16**   15 **35**   16 **42**   17 **90**

D Write as products of their prime factors.

| 18 | 2 × 2 × 7 |

18 28   21 100
19 36   22 50
20 32   23 63   24 56

E Write the prime factors common to each pair.

25 12 and 18
26 16 and 36
27 18 and 40
28 60 and 24
29 56 and 14
30 90 and 20

F Give the highest common factor.

| 31 | 7 |

31 28 and 35
32 12 and 30   35 12 and 68
33 16 and 28   36 32 and 56
34 18 and 42   37 36 and 63

G Give the lowest common multiple.

| 38 | 42 |

38 6 and 14
39 8 and 15   41 9 and 21
40 18 and 10   42 5 and 24

Challenge ☐☒

Play with 1, 2 or 3 partners. Use a dice and a counter for each player.

START	462	125	336	120	568	622	F
START	546	480	355	552	448	245	I N
START	342	333	240	156	224	537	I S
START	162	360	335	284	324	595	H

Each player chooses a coloured track and places a counter on START.
Take turns to roll the dice. If the dice number is a factor of the next number on the track, move to that section.
The first to the finish line wins.

A Find the three consecutive numbers that when added together make each total.

1 17, 18, 19

| 1 | 54 | 2 | 66 | 3 | 156 | 4 | 93 | 5 | 243 | 6 | 552 | 7 | 627 |

B Find the 4 consecutive numbers that when added together make each total.

| 8 | 94 | 10 | 166 | 12 | 238 | 14 | 566 |
| 9 | 70 | 11 | 150 | 13 | 346 | | |

D Copy and complete so that each calculation is correct.

17 230 ÷ 5 = 46

C Answer these.

15 Work out a formula for the sum of 3 consecutive odd numbers when the first number is a, the middle number b and the last number is c.

16 Work out a formula for the sum of 5 consecutive even numbers, a, b, c, d and e.

17 ⬟◼0 ÷ 5 = 4⬟

18 ⬜⬟4 ÷ 9 = 6◖

19
```
  ✴ 7 ●
 ×    7
 ─────────
 3 3 1 1
```

20
```
 2 ● ◼
 ×    4
 ─────────
 8 6 4
```

21 2◼6 × ◼★ = 8192

22 2▲ × 6◆◼ = 1512

23 ▲◼◻8 × 5◖ = 64 376

24 ●7● × 55 = ✴5 850

25 ●◼6✦ ÷ 8 = 5●8

26 37·◼ × 26 = ●◼5

27 43·●★ ÷ 9 = 4·◼4

Challenge — ×

a Using the key, work out any number less than 100 that could be represented by each flag. For example,

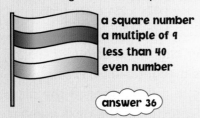

a square number
a multiple of 9
less than 40
even number

answer 36

Key

prime number
less than 40
greater than 80
square number
greater than 50
even number
odd number
multiple of 9
has 3 as a factor
sum of digits is 11
less than 70

A
E

B
F

C
G

D

b Make up some new flags. Test them out on a partner.

 Can you solve number puzzles and explain methods and reasoning?

Review 4

A Find the missing number.

1
```
   28·71
 − ▨▨▨▨
   12·92
```

3
```
   31·24
 − ▨▨▨▨
   16·65
```

2
```
   16·53
 − ▨▨▨▨
    6·66
```

4
```
   30·71
 − ▨▨▨▨
   17·08
```

B Answer these.

5 (15·26 + 7·83) − (28·07 − 17·64)
6 (23·74 − 7·26) + (23·85 − 12·7)
7 (52·63 + 11·68) − (6·24 + 7·98)

C Give the size of each missing angle without measuring.

8
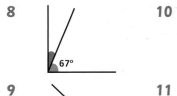
67°

9
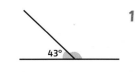
43°

10
75°

11

36°

D Find the perimeter and area of each shape.

12

8 m
9 m
3 m
17 m

13
6 m
3 m
4 m
14 m

14
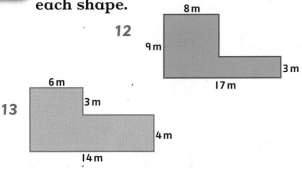
20 m
7 m
4 m
5 m   11 m

E Solve these problems.

15 How many 75 ml glasses can be filled from a bottle containing 0·6 l of water?

16 Which is the better value, 500 g of mushrooms for £1·60 or a 2 kg box of mushrooms for £6·25?

In a glass there is 200 ml of orange juice and 500 ml of water.

17 What is the proportion of orange juice in the glass?

18 What is the ratio of water to orange juice?

F Find the lowest common multiple for each pair.

19 6 and 15   21 4 and 22
20 8 and 18   22 5 and 16

G Give the prime factors.

23 **18**   24 **28**   25 **32**   26 **40**

H Give the highest common factor.

27 16 and 40   29 14 and 63
28 12 and 56   30 18 and 108

A Write the equivalent decimal.

1 $\frac{16}{100}$ 3 $\frac{2}{5}$ 5 $\frac{3}{4}$ 7 $\frac{4}{5}$

2 $\frac{3}{10}$ 4 $\frac{28}{100}$ 6 $\frac{11}{100}$

1 0·16

B Write the equivalent fraction.

8 $\frac{7}{10}$

8 0·7   10 0·3   12 0·25   14 0·75

9 0·6   11 0·9   13 0·1

C Write as a percentage.

15 $\frac{1}{5}$ 18 $\frac{3}{5}$ 21 $\frac{1}{4}$

15 20%

16 $\frac{7}{10}$ 19 $\frac{1}{2}$ 22 $\frac{4}{5}$

17 $\frac{9}{10}$ 20 $\frac{12}{100}$ 23 $\frac{72}{100}$

D Write the value of the red digit.

24 $\frac{8}{100}$

24 4·285   27 16·47

25 3·968   28 11·802

26 4·136   29 6·905   30 12·638

E Answer these.

31 3·64 × 10

32 4·25 ÷ 10   36 2·91 ÷ 10

33 26·2 × 100   37 476·3 ÷ 100

34 147·9 ÷ 100   38 3·024 × 100

35 3·75 × 100   39 64·17 × 10

F Write < or > to make each statement correct.

40 >

40 46·3 ● 4·36

41 4·26 ★ 42·6   44 71·24 ■ 72·4

42 24·36 ● 24·63   45 16·68 ● 16·81

43 11·89 ● 8·99   46 437 ■ 436·89

G Write in ascending order.

47 7·63 73 73·6 7·36 7·6

48 8·94 18·49 1·849 18·94 9·48

49 12·3 112·3 123·2 23·32 2·333

50 14·621 14·6 14·61 16·42 12·641

51 9·605 6·905 6·95 9·06 9·56

H Round to the nearest tenth.

52 14·86   54 19·43   56 16·583

53 15·49   55 2·551   57 12·471

Challenge

Follow the correct answers to find which fish is in danger from the shark.

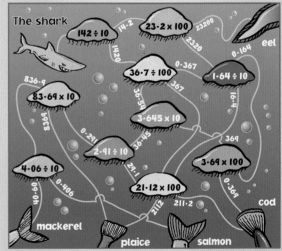

Design a trail like this for a partner.

A Copy and complete these sets of equivalent fractions.

$1\ \dfrac{2}{5} = \dfrac{4}{10} = \dfrac{8}{20} = \dfrac{10}{25}$

1 $\dfrac{2}{5} = \dfrac{4}{\bullet} = \dfrac{\bullet}{20} = \dfrac{10}{\bullet}$

2 $\dfrac{2}{3} = \dfrac{\bullet}{6} = \dfrac{8}{\blacktriangle} = \dfrac{10}{\bullet}$

3 $\dfrac{3}{10} = \dfrac{9}{\bullet} = \dfrac{\bullet}{40} = \dfrac{27}{\bullet}$

4 $\dfrac{2}{7} = \dfrac{\ast}{21} = \dfrac{12}{\ast} = \dfrac{20}{\bullet}$

5 $\dfrac{4}{9} = \dfrac{12}{\bigstar} = \dfrac{\bullet}{45} = \dfrac{32}{\bullet}$

6 $\dfrac{3}{8} = \dfrac{\bullet}{32} = \dfrac{\blacksquare}{40} = \dfrac{60}{\blacksquare}$

7 $\dfrac{2}{11} = \dfrac{4}{\bullet} = \dfrac{\blacksquare}{88} = \dfrac{200}{\bigstar}$

8 $\dfrac{5}{9} = \dfrac{\bigstar}{27} = \dfrac{25}{\bullet} = \dfrac{5000}{\bullet}$

B Write a common factor for the numerator and denominator for each fraction.

9 $\dfrac{15}{24}$ 11 $\dfrac{27}{72}$ 13 $\dfrac{32}{52}$

10 $\dfrac{14}{35}$ 12 $\dfrac{16}{56}$

C Write each fraction in its lowest terms.

$14\ \dfrac{3}{5}$

14 $\dfrac{12}{20}$ 17 $\dfrac{9}{12}$

15 $\dfrac{15}{50}$ 18 $\dfrac{32}{80}$ 20 $\dfrac{20}{85}$

16 $\dfrac{16}{28}$ 19 $\dfrac{12}{66}$ 21 $\dfrac{48}{108}$ 22 $\dfrac{64}{176}$

D Solve these problems.

23 $\dfrac{3}{10}$ of Amy's money is £27. How much money does she have altogether?

24 Andy spends $\dfrac{2}{5}$ of his money and has £18 left. How much did he spend?

25 After travelling 474 km Oscar has completed $\dfrac{3}{8}$ of his journey to the South Pole. How much further must he travel to complete all of the journey?

26 A sheepdog has rounded up $\dfrac{3}{7}$ of the farmer's sheep. If there are still 40 sheep to round up, how many sheep does the farmer have?

Challenge ▬ ☒

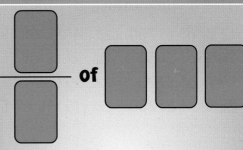

Play with a partner. Use a calculator, number cards 1 to 9 and a large copy of this grid.

Shuffle the cards and place them face down. In turn, take the top card and place it on one of the grid sections. Place the next card in the same way and continue until the grid is complete. Work out your answer to the nearest whole number. The higher number scores a point. First to 10 points wins the game.

Can you reduce a fraction to its lowest terms and find fractions of numbers and quantities?

87

A Write as a decimal and as a fraction in its lowest terms.

1 0·24 $\frac{6}{25}$

1	24%	3	28%	5	48%	7	72%	9	5%
2	32%	4	16%	6	35%	8	15%	10	12%

11   4%

B Find how far each car has travelled.

12   15% of 480 miles

13   45% of 360 miles

14   81% of 600 miles

15   22% of 450 miles

C Find each amount. Estimate first. Use a calculator.

16	12% of £2200	20	49% of £3000
17	74% of £450	21	$2\frac{1}{2}$% of £680
18	99% of £700	22	$17\frac{1}{2}$% of £5000
19	26% of £1200	23	151% of £6000

D Solve these problems.

24 In a fishing competition Jim Pike catches 50 fish. If 32% are roach and 12% are perch, how many fish are not roach or perch?

25 The cost of a car is £3648·25 plus $17\frac{1}{2}$% tax. What is the total cost of the car, to the nearest penny?

26 A chef cooks 150 cakes. 24 are chocolate, 8 are lemon and the rest are fruit cakes. To the nearest whole number, what percentage are fruit cakes?

E Find the percentage to the nearest whole number.

27	24 out of 37	31	32 out of 49
28	15 out of 42	32	74 out of 77
29	17 out of 47	33	96 out of 112
30	12 out of 106	34	89 out of 220

Challenge

VAT adds 17·5% to the cost of these items. Work out the VAT on each item to the nearest penny.

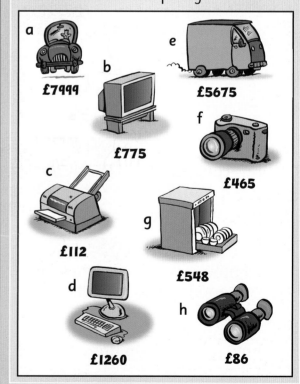

a £7999

b £775

c £112

d £1260

e £5675

f £465

g £548

h £86

Can you find simple percentages of small whole number quantities?

A Answer these. Use column addition.

1 4652 + 439
2 7604 + 1329
3 207 + 1983

4 5216 + 742
5 635 + 1284 + 26

B Answer these. Use column subtraction.

6 4293 − 1462
7 5391 − 864
8 1234 − 438

9 9082 − 3654
10 7649 − 168
11 6421 − 1964

C Answer these.

12 6 × 9
13 4 × 8
14 7 × 6

15 9 × 8
16 8 × 8
17 9 × 5

18 9 × 9
19 7 × 8
20 7 × 7

D Find the answer, showing your working. Estimate first. Write (H) by the answer if you can work it out in your head.

21 738 + 429

22 14·6 + 19·84 + 0·68

23 3009 − 368

24 386·27 + 39·08 + 6·2

25 6008 − 173

26 2006 + 996

27 347·4 − 2·69

28 54·2 − 13·95

29 321·96 + 18·5 + 0·07

30 8005 − 994

31 521·63 − 138·9

32 630·1 − 59·48

Challenge

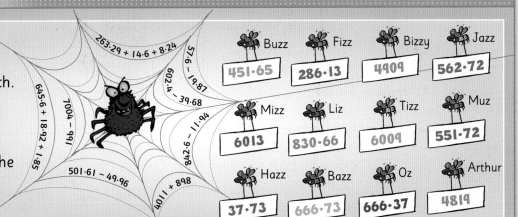

Work out which flies the spider will catch.

Make up web questions for the flies that are not caught.

263·29 + 14·6 + 8·24
57·6 − 19·87
602·14 − 39·68
645·6 + 18·92 + 1·85
7004 − 1961
842·6 − 11·94
501·61 − 49·96
4011 + 898

Buzz 451·65
Fizz 286·13
Bizzy 4909
Jazz 562·72
Mizz 6013
Liz 830·66
Tizz 6009
Muz 551·72
Hazz 37·73
Bazz 666·73
Oz 666·37
Arthur 4819

Can you use column addition and column subtraction for numbers involving decimals?

89

A Find each answer, showing your working. Approximate first.

1 6423 × 4
2 4137 × 6
3 1594 × 5
4 3624 × 8

5 2468 × 9
6 2316 × 7
7 4836 × 6
8 6213 × 5

B Show how to check the answer.

9 to question 1
10 to question 5

C Answer these. Use the information in the tool box.

11 10 980 ÷ 5
12 1220 × 0·9
13 21·96 × 5
14 358·4 × 3
15 10 752 ÷ 7
16 15·36 × 7
17 358·4 × 0·3
18 219·6 × 0·5

19 10 980 ÷ 1220

```
1536 × 7 = 10752
1220 × 9 = 10980
2196 × 5 = 10980
3584 × 3 = 10752
```

D Answer these.

20 515 × 26
21 427 × 13
22 526 × 37

E Use your answers to questions 20, 21 and 22 to answer these.

23 51·5 × 26
24 5·26 × 37
25 42·7 × 1·3
26 51·5 × 2·6

27 427 × 0·13
28 52·6 × 3·7
29 515 × 260
30 52·6 × 370

F Use this information to answer these.

68 × 4 = 272

31 168 × 4
32 6·8 × 4
33 68 × 14
34 68 × 5
35 6·8 × 0·4
36 68 × 1·4

G Answer these. Some have a remainder.

37 4364 ÷ 4
38 5291 ÷ 5
39 736 ÷ 8

40 1423 ÷ 7
41 865 ÷ 9
42 1629 ÷ 9

Challenge

Play with a partner. Use number cards 1 to 9 and 2 sets of 12 counters. Take turns to shuffle the cards. Lay the top 4 down to make a 4-digit number. Turn over a fifth card. Multiply the 4-digit number by the number on the fifth card. If the thousand digit in your answer is on the grid, cover it with a counter. For example, 2437 × 6 = 14 622 so cover 4. Place only 1 counter at each turn. The winner is the first to place all 12 counters.

8	4	5	2	2
6	1	3	2	5
4	9	1	7	8
0	3	9	3	5
4	7	0	1	6

Can you understand and use short multiplication of numbers involving decimals and short division?

A Find each answer, showing your working. Approximate first.

1 144 ÷ 8
2 243 ÷ 9
3 138 ÷ 6
4 272 ÷ 8

5 224 ÷ 7
6 230 ÷ 5

7 405 ÷ 9
8 294 ÷ 7

E Write a 'number story' for each statement.

> 28 When a motorway that is 24·6 miles long is extended by 8·54 miles, the total length of the motorway is 33·14 miles.

B Use your answers to the questions above to answer these.

9 144 ÷ 0·8
10 138 ÷ 0·6
11 24·3 ÷ 9

12 29·4 ÷ 7
13 405 ÷ 0·9

28 24·6 + 8·54 = 33·14
29 51·62 + 4·9 = 56·52
30 8·25 × 3·6 = 29·7
31 142·8 − 6·36 = 136·44
32 116·84 ÷ 46 = 2·54

C Answer these.

14 58·8 ÷ 3
15 47·6 ÷ 7
16 324 ÷ 0·6
17 568 ÷ 0·4

18 30·5 ÷ 5
19 639 ÷ 0·9
20 42·4 ÷ 8
21 592 ÷ 0·4

D Answer these. Use a calculator.

22 21·46 ÷ ● = 5·8
23 16·575 ÷ ▲ = 3·9
24 25·024 ÷ 3·68 = ●
25 ◆ ÷ 2·6 = 8·45
26 71·68 ÷ ● = 2·8
27 45·243 ÷ ● = 4·57

F Answer these.

33 6·54 × 6
34 4·18 × 7
35 2·93 × 8
36 4·72 × 4
37 13·64 × 9
38 21·83 × 6

39 42·44 ÷ 4
40 73·85 ÷ 5
41 33·75 ÷ 9
42 41·76 ÷ 6
43 42·84 ÷ 7

Challenge

In a magic square the sum of the numbers in any line – horizontal, vertical and diagonal – is the same. Copy and complete these magic squares.

a

2·72		5·44
9·52		
8·16		10·88

b

32·88		10·96
		49·32
	16·44	21·92

c

13·14		2·92	
5·11	8·76	9·49	7·3
	5·84		10·22
4·38			2·19

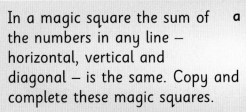

Can you use mental, calculator or pencil and paper methods to support, record or explain calculations?

91

A Work out each area.

1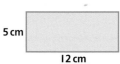
11 cm
4 cm

2
20 cm
15 cm

3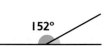
5 cm
12 cm

D Measure these for this shape.

16 the longest side in mm
17 the shortest side in mm
18 each angle to the nearest degree

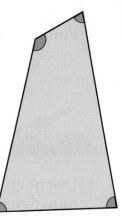

B Find each missing angle without measuring.

4 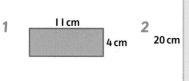 152°

6 136°

5 76°

7 39°

E Draw each triangle to the actual size. Measure the two missing angles and the length of the third side.

19  7 cm 55° 9 cm

20 8 cm 10 cm

21 7.5 cm 62° 5 cm

C Copy and complete.

	Fraction of a complete turn	Amount of turn in degrees
8	$\frac{1}{2}$	180°
9	$\frac{1}{3}$	
10	$\frac{1}{4}$	
11	$\frac{1}{5}$	
12	$\frac{1}{6}$	
13	$\frac{1}{10}$	
14	$\frac{2}{3}$	
15	$\frac{3}{4}$	

Challenge ▬ ✕

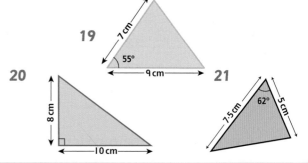

Find the missing angles. Do not use a protractor.
The green shapes are isosceles triangles. The yellow shape is an equilateral triangle. The pink shape is a square. The blue shape is a rectangle.

 Can you use a protractor to measure and draw angles to the nearest degree?

A

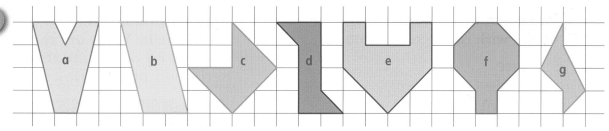

1 Which shapes have reflective symmetry?

B Copy each shape and the mirror line onto squared paper. Draw the reflection of each shape in the mirror line.

2

3

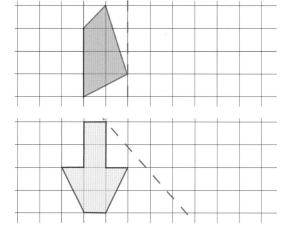

C Copy the shape and the mirror lines onto squared paper. Reflect the shape in the 2 mirror lines.

4

D Write which of these shapes are:

5 reflections of the start shape
6 translations of the start shape.

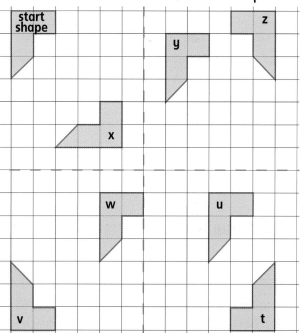

Challenge ▢▢✕

Using the diagram in D, write instructions to translate or reflect the start shape to move it to the position of:

a shape z   **c** shape w   **e** shape v
b shape y   **d** shape u   **f** shape t.

Can you recognize where a simple shape will be after 2 translations or 2 reflections?

93

A On cm-squared paper draw each shape with an area of $16\,\text{cm}^2$.

1 a square
2 a triangle
3 3 different rectangles
4 a trapezium
5 a parallelogram

B These shapes have been drawn on cm-squared paper. Find the perimeter of these shapes in the sequence.

6 40 cm

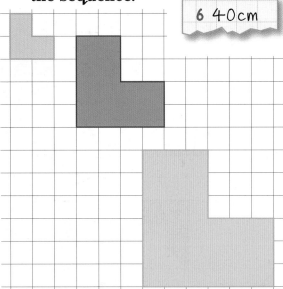

6 5th shape   8 10th shape
7 6th shape   9 100th shape

C This garden has a lawn and flower beds. Work out the area covered by grass and the perimeter of each flower bed.

10

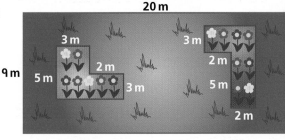

D Using the sequence of L shapes in B, work out the area of each shape

11 2nd shape   15 10th shape
12 3rd shape   16 20th shape
13 4th shape   17 100th shape
14 5th shape

E Find the size of the missing angles. Do not use a protractor.

18

20

19

21

Challenge   − ☒

Each diagram is a net of a cube. The base is shaded and the top face of the cube is marked with a T. On squared paper draw as many different nets of cubes as you can, with the bases shaded and the top faces marked with a T.

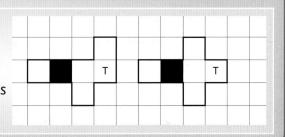

Can you calculate the perimeter and area of simple compound shapes?

You need: ● 38 counters

Cover the answers to the questions on the canoes in order on the grids below.
When you complete a column write down the letter of that column.
Work out the hidden message and answer the question.

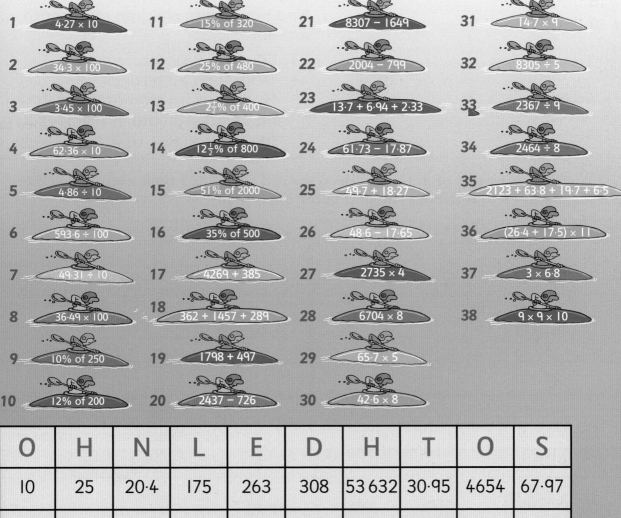

1 4.27×10
2 34.3×100
3 3.45×100
4 62.36×10
5 $4.86 \div 10$
6 $593.6 \div 100$
7 $49.31 \div 10$
8 36.49×100
9 10% of 250
10 12% of 200

11 15% of 320
12 25% of 480
13 $2\frac{1}{2}\%$ of 400
14 $12\frac{1}{2}\%$ of 800
15 51% of 2000
16 35% of 500
17 $4269 + 385$
18 $362 + 1457 + 289$
19 $1798 + 497$
20 $2437 - 726$

21 $8307 - 1649$
22 $2004 - 799$
23 $13.7 + 6.94 + 2.33$
24 $61.73 - 17.87$
25 $49.7 + 18.27$
26 $48.6 - 17.65$
27 2735×4
28 6704×8
29 65.7×5
30 42.6×8

31 14.7×9
32 $8305 \div 5$
33 $2367 \div 9$
34 $2464 \div 8$
35 $2123 + 63.8 + 19.7 + 6.5$
36 $(26.4 + 17.5) \times 11$
37 3×6.8
38 $9 \times 9 \times 10$

O	H	N	L	E	D	H	T	O	S
10	25	20.4	175	263	308	53 632	30.95	4654	67.97
24	623.6	328.5	120	6658	42.7	2295	5.936	100	4.931

E	R	N	L	I	G	I	W	E
132.3	1661	1711	2213	43.86	1205	482.9	1020	810
10 940	3430	2108	3649	48	345	22.97	0.486	340.8

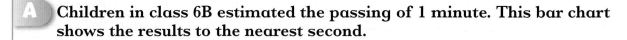
A Children in class 6B estimated the passing of 1 minute. This bar chart shows the results to the nearest second.

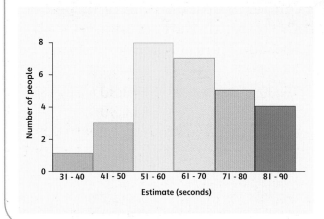

1 Give a title for the bar chart.
2 Find how many children are in the class.

Find how many children made each estimate.

3 50 seconds or less
4 more than 80 seconds
5 Find what fraction of the children made an estimate in the 51–60 seconds range.

B Working in teams of 4, the children scored points for their estimates. Use these tables to work out the points for each team.

Estimate (seconds)	Points
31–40	1
41–50	2
51–60	3
61–70	3
71–80	2
81–90	1

	Team	Estimates (seconds)
6	A	46 60 81 58
7	B	85 59 82 62
8	C	70 66 50 55
9	D	64 52 80 73
10	E	52 76 75 63
11	F	89 49 62 68
12	G	57 71 55 39

Challenge ▢☒

Use a stop-watch. Ask the children in your class to estimate the passing of 1 minute. Time each estimate with a stop-watch. Record your results.
Draw a bar chart with grouped data to show your results.

Can you solve a problem by representing, extracting and interpreting data in tables, graphs and charts?

A The blue line shows Mr Retour's car journey.
The red line shows Eileen Dover's motorcycle ride.
Use the graph and chart to answer each question.

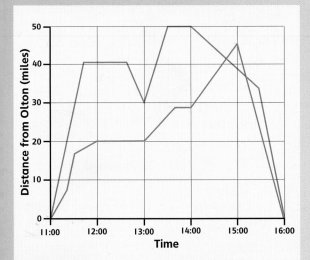

Say approximately how far Mr Retour
was from Olton at each time.

1	15:00	3	13:30
2	12:00	4	11:30

Say approximately how far Eileen was
from Olton after riding for each amount
of time.

5 $\frac{1}{2}$ hour   6 $\frac{3}{4}$ hour

7 Mr Retour spent 20 minutes in
Arlford. At what time did he leave
Arlford?

8 At approximately what time did
Eileen stop for a rest in Balby?

9 When Eileen left Balby after her
rest, how far from Olton was
Mr Retour?

10 Eileen passed through Blay twice.
At approximately what times did
she do this?

11 Eileen saw Mr Retour in Barnham. At
approximately what time was this?

Town	Distance from Olton
Arlford	28 miles
Balby	41 miles
Blay	45 miles
Barnham	37 miles

B This pie chart represents the
colours of counters in a bag.
If there are 48 counters in the
bag find how many are:

12 yellow
13 blue
14 red
15 orange.

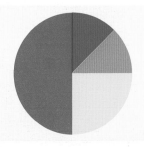

Challenge

Shuffle a pack of playing cards.
Turn over the top 8 cards.
Draw a pie chart to represent the number
of hearts, clubs,
diamonds and spades
you have turned over.
Try again with 12 cards.

Can you solve a problem by extracting and interpreting data in line
graphs and pie charts?

97

A Use the conversion graph to answer these. Find approximately how many Hong Kong dollars you would get for each amount.

1 £1
2 £4
3 £6
4 £4·50
5 £7·50
6 £14

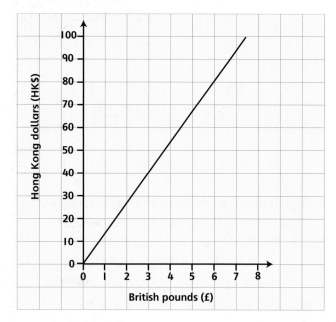

Hong Kong dollars (HK$) / British pounds (£)

B Give the range, mode, median and mean for each set of scores in the archery contest.

7	Geoff	6	1	4	7	8	1	4	5	9	
8	Carol	7	7	3	7	6	4	8	3	9	
9	George	8	9	3	7	6	2	2	7	1	
10	Jenny	5	6	7	6	7	5	5	4	9	

C Solve these problems.

11 In a sale all items are reduced by 20%. How much does John save when he buys 2 books for £7·50 and £12·80?

12 Mike saves 20p and 5p coins in a bottle. He has 125 5p coins. The total value of the coins in the bottle is £46·25. How many 20p coins has he saved?

A fairground ride costs £5·10 for an adult and 3 children and £6·90 for an adult and 5 children. Find the cost for:

13 1 child
14 1 adult.

Challenge

The unit of currency in Thailand is the baht. 68 bahts have the same value as £1.

a Draw a conversion graph on cm-squared paper to show how many bahts you would receive for amounts up to £10.

b Write 10 questions for a partner to answer by using your graph.

Can you identify and use appropriate operations to solve word problems involving numbers and quantities based on 'real life' or money?

A Solve these problems:

1 A container holds 50 boxes of mobile phones. There are 12 phones in each box. If 8 boxes are taken from the container, how many phones will be left in the container?

2 If a machine produces a box of chocolates every 12 seconds, how many boxes can it produce in 8 hours?

B Look at the conversion scale. Find the approximate temperature in °F when the temperature is:

3 ⁻8°C   6 8°C
4 18°C   7 ⁻3°C
5 ⁻2°C   8 16°C

Temperature conversions

°C	°F
20	68
15	59
10	50
5	41
0	32
−5	23
−10	14

Arrange these temperatures in order, warmest first.

9 12°C, 47°F, 22°F, ⁻3°C, 1°C
10 15°F, 15°C, 41°F, 4°C, 51°F

C Approximate each length in inches.

11 8·9 cm   13 3·8 cm   15 7·3 cm
12 12·1 cm   14 11·1 cm

D Peppercorns cost £1·30 for 50 g. Write how much each mass costs.

16 20 g   19 100 g   21 ½ kg
17 30 g   20 300 g   22 2 kg
18 75 g

Challenge ⊟ ⊠

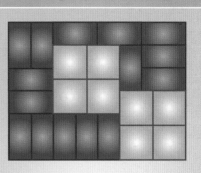

In this garden each turf is a rectangle with a breadth that is half its length. Each paving slab is a square.

a What is the length of each turf if the length of the garden is 4·68 m?

b What is the length of each side of a paving slab if the breadth of a turf is 30 cm?

c What is the area of each turf if the breadth of the garden is 2·16 m?

d What is the area of each paving slab if the garden is 3·84 m in length?

e Make up 3 more questions about the garden for a partner.

Can you identify appropriate operations to solve word problems involving measures?

99

A Solve these problems.

Milk fudge
280 ml milk
400 g sugar
80 g butter
2 ml vanilla essence

Town	Train 1	Train 2	Train 3
Beeton	10:55	12:36	14:27
Stowe	11:20	12:58	14:51
Cranby	11:35	13:12	15:07
Porby	11:54	13:29	15:25

This recipe for milk fudge is enough for 40 pieces. Find how much milk you would need to make:

1 60 pieces of fudge
2 100 pieces of fudge
3 25 pieces of fudge
4 220 pieces of fudge.

Find how much butter you will need if you use:

5 100 g of sugar
6 600 g of sugar
7 250 g of sugar.

Find how much vanilla essence you will need if you use:

8 200 g of butter
9 700 ml of milk.

10 How long does train 3 take to travel from Stowe to Porby?
11 Which train takes the least amount of time for the whole journey?
12 Emma travelled from Beeton to Cranby on train 2. For how long was she travelling?
13 Flo arrives at Beeton station at 11:45 a.m. How long will she have to wait for a train?
14 Dave is travelling on train 3, which is on time. This is the time on Dave's watch. Where is he?
15 Alison arrives at Cranby station at 14:26 to catch the train to Porby. How long will it be before she arrives in Porby?

Challenge

Play with a partner. Use 2 sets of 8 counters, a dice and a large copy of the number grid. Place a counter on the start. Take turns to roll the dice and move the counter around the track. Answer the question in each section by taking the dice number as the value of n. For example, for 2n + 3 and dice [5], the answer is 11.

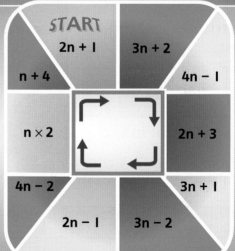

START
2n + 1
3n + 2
n + 4
4n − 1
n × 2
2n + 3
4n − 2
3n + 1
2n − 1
3n − 2

16	23	11	13	2
18	1	7	15	3
12	5	11	4	22
7	6	5	19	8
14	20	10	17	9

If your answer is on the grid, cover it with a counter. The first to place all 8 counters wins the game.

Can you solve problems involving ratio and proportion?

A Write a formula for the nth term in each sequence.

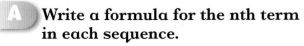

1   4, 6, 8, 10, 12, 14, …
2   5, 8, 11, 14, 17, …
3   7, 12, 17, 22, 27, …

B Explain your answer to each question.

4   Will the number 99 be in this sequence?
    4, 7, 10, 13, 16, …
5   Will the number 1760 be in this sequence?
    80, 160, 240, 320, 400, …

C A number is hidden by each coloured circle. Use the clues to find each hidden number.

6   If I increase the number under the red circle by $\frac{1}{5}$ the answer is 30.

7   The sum of the numbers under the brown and yellow circles is 135. The brown circle number is 43 greater than the yellow one.

8   The number under the orange circle is 80% of the number under the red circle.

9   The difference between the number under the pink circle and the number under the brown circle is 8. The number under the pink circle is a square number.

10 The numbers under the black and blue circles are both prime numbers. Their product is 2 less than the brown circle number. The black circle number is

11 smaller than the blue circle number.

12 If you add together all the hidden numbers the answer is 293.

D Work out the numbers represented by m and n in each pair of statements.

13   $m = 9$
     $n = 3$

13   $m + n = 12$
     $m - n = 6$
14   $m \times n = 42$
     $m - n = 1$
15   $2m + n = 16$
     $n \div m = 2$
16   $3m - 3 = n$
     $m \times n = 36$

17   $m \times 9 = n \times 12$
     $m + 2n = 10$
18   $5m = n + 7$
     $m \times n = 24$
19   $2m + 2n = 34$
     $n - m = {}^{-}1$

Challenge — ×

$E \times T = 15$

$1232 \div H = 154$

$N^2 - 4 = 12$

$R \times F = 42$

$(M \times F) + A = 54$

$I \times I \times I = 1$

$3M - 6 = 3R$

$M \times M = 81$

$E + 3I = 6$ $E + T = 8$

$22 - 3S = 16$

Use these clues to work out the number represented by each letter. Work out the hidden message.

Highly confidential
(use specified code)

9335 05 583 257309
05 58733 6165334

Can you express a relationship in symbols and start to use simple formulae?

101

This is the Jolly family. Mr and Mrs Jolly are taking their 3 children on a day trip.

Follow their journey and answer the questions.

Kenton

Leave Kenton at 08:44

Arrive home 22:17

Kelsey

Arrive 10:15
Leave 11:19

1 Mr and Mrs Jolly had 1 ride at the fair, their children had 2 rides. What was the total cost?

Kelsey Fair Rides
Adults £2·30
Children 85p

Arrive 11:58
Leave 12:24

Stanton

Salcombe

Arrive 18:44
Leave 21:16

5 The children's aunt is cooking a meal. Her jam tart recipe is for 3 people. Re-write the recipe for 7 people.

Jam tarts
Plain flour	75 g
Butter	45 g
Water	3 tablespoons
Jam	6 teaspoons

Slofield

Arrive 12:58
Leave 14:05

2 Mr Jolly's car was in the car park during their visit. How much did this cost?

Slofield car park charges
Up to 1 hour 80p
Up to 2 hours £1·70
More than 2 hours £5

Milton Bowling Tournament

Milton

Arrive 14:52
Leave 16:03

6 For how long was the family out?

7 For how long was Mr Jolly driving?

8 What was the total distance travelled?

9 Where was the longest stop?

10 Where was the shortest stop?

11 Which graph represents the journey? Explain your answer.

3 These are the family's scores in the bowling tournament. Find the range, mode, median and mean for each set of scores.

Mr Jolly	4	6	4	8	4	3	6
Mrs Jolly	3	5	3	5	0	7	5
Kevin	6	6	3	10	3	3	4
Ben	6	2	5	2	5	2	6
Liz	9	2	4	3	9	4	4

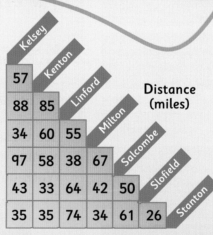

Distance (miles)

Kelsey					
57	Kenton				
88	85	Linford			
34	60	55	Milton		
97	58	38	67	Salcombe	
43	33	64	42	50	Slofield
35	35	74	34	61	26	Stanton

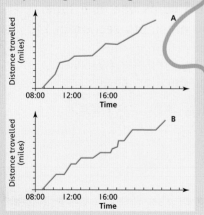

A

Distance travelled (miles)

08:00   12:00   16:00
Time

B

Distance travelled (miles)

08:00   12:00   16:00
Time

Linford

Arrive 17:07
Leave 17:38

4 These are the things that the family bought at Linford sale. Work out the cost of each item.

LINFORD SALE
40% off everything

ROAD ATLAS

£15·90
£8·60
£55·25
£18·60
£29·45

A Write in order, smallest first.

1 4·62 2·46 6·24 4·26 4·66
2 3·71 3·07 3·77 3·17 1·37
3 11·95 11·59 15·91 19·15 11·55
4 24·23 23·42 23·24 23·32 24·32
5 19·99 20·19 20·91 19·19 19·91
6 18·43 18·33 18·44 18·34 13·84

B Answer these.

7 9×7 10 7×7 13 7×8
8 6×7 11 6×8 14 9×9
9 8×9 12 6×6 15 8×4

C For each machine, work out the operations carried out on the input numbers to get the output number.

16

Yellow card	Blue card	Output
3	2	9
2	3	11
5	7	26
0	4	12
8	6	26

17

Orange card	Blue card	Output
5	4	7
7	2	17
1	3	⁻3
7	6	9
10	1	28

18

Pink card	Blue card	Orange card	Output
1	4	5	16
2	0	4	10
5	4	3	26
7	2	0	25
8	1	6	32

Challenge ▬ ✕

Play with a partner. Use number cards 0 to 9, a dice, a counter and a large copy of the grid below.
Take turns to roll the dice and count around the track.

| START | 75·04 | 47·15 |
| 52·65 59·78 | 85·96 | 56·25 |

| 14·06 19·23 | | 15·62 24·35 |

| 22·61 34·72 | **Score 5 points to win** | 24·02 34·96 |

| 85·62 96·11 | | 74·85 82·63 |

| 76·85 87·92 | | 12·64 23·82 |

| 47·63 53·42 | 62·43 71·24 | 56·21 63·14 |

Try to form a number on the grid that lies between the 2 numbers in the section on the track.
Shuffle the cards, turn the top card over and place it on any section of the grid.
Turn the next 3 cards one at a time.
Place them on an empty section of the grid.
If your grid number lies between the 2 track numbers score a point.
First to score 5 points wins the game.

Can you solve a problem by extracting and interpreting information presented in tables?

103

A

Write 2 whole number division facts and 4 decimal division facts linked to each statement.

1 $9 \times 5 = 45$
2 $6 \times 7 = 42$
3 $7 \times 5 = 35$
4 $4 \times 8 = 32$
5 $6 \times 9 = 54$
6 $6 \times 5 = 30$

1 $4.5 \div 9 = 5$ $4.5 \div 9 = 0.5$
   $4.5 \div 5 = 9$ $4.5 \div 0.5 = 90$
   $4.5 \div 0.9 = 50$ $4.5 \div 5 = 0.9$

7 $9 \times 3 = 27$
8 $6 \times 4 = 24$
9 $8 \times 1 = 8$
10 $10 \times 6 = 60$

B

Write in order, smallest first.

11 3·6 3·52 3·25 3·521 3·125

12 4·26 4·6 4·65 4·263 4·362

13 8·91 8·2 9·182 9·28 9·028

14 11·651 11·7 11·607 11·72 11·272

15 8·601 8·061 8·16 8·61 8·66

C

Study the football league tables.

2003

Team	Won	Lost	Drawn	Goals scored	Points
Rovers	8	0	2	22	26
Rangers	8	2	0	36	24
United	6	2	2	21	20
Diamonds	5	5	0	17	15
Kings	1	9	0	7	3
Valley	0	10	0	12	0

2004

Team	Won	Lost	Drawn	Goals scored	Points
United	8	2	0	24	40
Kings	5	1	4	23	37
Rangers	7	1	2	20	36
Rovers	2	7	1	18	23
Valley	4	6	0	14	22
Diamonds	0	9	1	9	10

16 How were points awarded in 2003?
17 How were points awarded in 2004?
18 If the points in 2003 had been awarded in the same way as 2004, in what order would the teams have finished?

If 4 points had been given for a win, 2 points for a draw and 2 points for every 5 goals scored, find which team would have:

19 won the league in 2003
20 come 4th in the league in 2004.

Challenge

Find the smallest number in:
a column 2
b row 3
c column 5
d on the whole grid.

4·67	3·64	3·47	4·82	6·24
3·85	9·29	9·82	6·73	6·63
9·62	1·07	8·04	9·65	2·95
6·43	3·76	7·96	3·91	7·82
8·75	4·83	7·38	8·07	8·63

Find the largest number in:
e column 4 **f** row 5 **g** row 1
h on the whole grid.

i If the numbers in each column are added together, predict which column will have the highest total.

j If the numbers in each row are added together, predict which row will have the smallest total.

k Check your predictions.

Can you order a mixed set of numbers with up to 3 decimal places?

A   Solve these problems.

Car	Power steering	Antilock brakes	Metallic paint*	0–60 mph time (secs)	Number of seats	Miles per gallon	Size of engine	Cost
Laser	✓	✓	✓	7·9	2	25	2·5 l	£25 200
Macro	✓	✗	✓	11·2	4	35	1·4 l	£9450
Goa	✓	✓	✓	9·8	3	33	2·0 l	£13 440
Dart	✓	✓	✗	8·6	3	30	2·3 l	£14 640
Banga	✓	✓	✗	13·6	5	38	1·1 l	£6999

*metallic paint £350 extra   Other extras: spoiler £525, alloy wheels £480

1 Which car has an engine smaller than 1·6 l and costs less than £8000?

2 Which cars have antilock brakes, power steering and will travel more than 30 miles per gallon?

3 Find the cost of a Banga with a spoiler and alloy wheels.

4 Which car has power steering, metallic paint, 4 or more seats and travels more than 30 miles per gallon?

5 Which car will reach 60 mph in less than 10 seconds, has metallic paint and costs less than £20 000?

6 Find the cost of each car when $17\frac{1}{2}$% VAT is added.

7 Find the cost of each car when prices are reduced by 15% in a sale.

Challenge

45 ÷ 0·5	100 ÷ 25	6·4 ÷ 8	3·6 ÷ 3·6	2·8 ÷ 7
36 ÷ 0·9	5·6 ÷ 8	40 ÷ 8	1·8 ÷ 9	36 ÷ 6
81 ÷ 9	49 ÷ 0·7	300 ÷ 100	6·3 ÷ 7	25 ÷ 0·5
72 ÷ 0·9	56 ÷ 7	3·5 ÷ 7	80 ÷ 40	2·7 ÷ 9
42 ÷ 6	24 ÷ 1·2	24 ÷ 0·8	30 ÷ 0·5	4·2 ÷ 7

Player 2

90	40	9	0·4	0·6
3	0·7	60	4	80
0·8	2	0·9	7	0·2
6	50	30	1	20
70	5	0·3	8	0·5

Player 1   Player 1

Player 2

Play with a partner. Use 25 counters and a large copy of each grid. Put a counter in each rectangle in the division grid. Take turns to remove a counter and answer the question beneath. Place the counter on the square with the correct answer. The first to link their zones with a pathway of counters is the winner.

Can you solve a problem by extracting and interpreting information presented in tables, graphs and charts?

105

A Answer these. Use a column method.

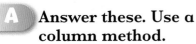

1 3268 + 1475
2 1439 + 2468
3 5276 + 3924
4 1896 + 6627
5 2675 + 3684
6 4006 + 8754
7 3095 + 8672
8 9876 + 6789
9 4203 − 1127

10 6027 − 4168
11 3002 − 1786
12 4403 − 3294
13 8060 − 4236
14 5437 − 1987
15 6431 − 1366
16 9021 − 3376

B Answer these. Use column addition.

17 7·492 + 1·639
18 11·63 + 8·507
19 46·2 + 38·43
20 19·751 + 2·6

21 24·203 + 7·02
22 37·66 + 19·247
23 136·43 + 2·974
24 7·3 + 18·648

C Answer these. Use column subtraction.

25 27·624 − 18·342
26 17·95 − 2·861
27 13·68 − 8·463
28 19 − 6·248
29 12·3 − 7·594
30 21·96 − 14·234
31 18 − 6·145
32 216·2 − 17·951

D Check your answers to these questions. Show your working.

33 question 18
34 question 21
35 question 24

36 question 26
37 question 29
38 question 32

E Find which two cards were put into the machine to get each output.

Input cards

14·7	6·324	6·543
15·79	13·43	6·52
14·25	8·2	7·75

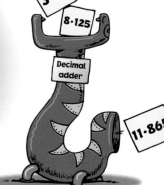

3·74
8·125
Decimal adder
11·865

39 21·243
40 21·18
41 12·844

42 30·04
43 14·27

44 21·63
45 13·063

Challenge ▭ ✕

Copy and complete each magic square. The sum of the 3 numbers in a horizontal, vertical or diagonal line must be the same.

a

13·35		
2·225	11·125	20·025
	6·675	

b

26·568	3·321	19·926
9·963		
13·284		

c

13·35	42·275	44·5	20·025
		24·475	
28·925		33·375	22·25
40·05	15·575		

Can you carry out column addition and subtraction of numbers involving decimals?

A Solve these problems.

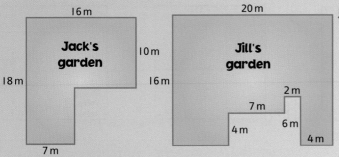

Jack's garden — 16 m, 10 m, 18 m, 16 m, 7 m

Jill's garden — 20 m, 16 m, 2 m, 7 m, 4 m, 6 m, 4 m

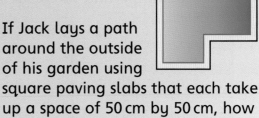

Find the area of:

1 Jack's garden
2 Jill's garden.
3 If Jack digs 2 rectangular flower beds in his garden measuring 12 m by $3\frac{1}{2}$ m and 9 m by 11 m and then lays turf on the rest of the garden, what is the area covered by turf?
4 Jill sows grass over all her garden. Grass seed costs 42p per square metre. What is the cost of seed for the whole garden?

5 If Jack lays a path around the outside of his garden using square paving slabs that each take up a space of 50 cm by 50 cm, how many paving slabs will he need? (Don't forget the corners!)
6 What will be the perimeter of Jack's garden measured around the outside of the path?
7 If paving slabs cost £1·78 each, how much will Jack pay for his path?
8 Jill wants to put a fence around her garden. Fencing costs £3·20 per metre. How much will Jill's fencing cost?
9 Jill has agreed to give half of her garden to her brother. Draw some sketches on squared paper to show how she could divide her garden.

Challenge

a On cm-squared paper design an interesting shaped garden. Each side must be a number of whole squares.
b If the side of each square on your plan represents a length of 1 m, work out the perimeter of your garden.

c If you laid paving slabs, like the ones used by Jack, around the outside of your garden, how many paving slabs would you need?
d How much would the slabs cost you at £1·78 each?
e If you put up a fence around your garden at a cost of £3·20 per metre, what would be the cost of your fence?

Can you calculate the perimeter and area of simple compound shapes?

A

Each square has been split into rectangles. Find the length of the sides of each rectangle and the area of each square.

1

40 cm²
24 cm²

2

16 cm²	12 cm²
8 cm²	

3

18 cm²	
	28 cm²

4

30 m²	18 m²

B

Use Multilink cubes.

5 Copy each net onto cm-squared paper. Cut out each net. Fold the paper and stick the flaps to make an open box.

6 Find how many Multilink cubes the yellow box will hold.

7 Find how many Multilink cubes the green box will hold.

8 Without making the box, find how many Multilink cubes the orange box will hold. Explain your answer.

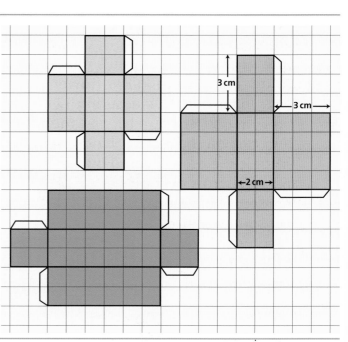

3 cm

3 cm

2 cm

C

Work out the surface area of each cuboid.

9

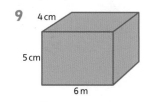

4 cm
5 cm
6 m

10

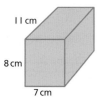

11 cm
8 cm
7 cm

11

80 cm²
40 cm²
10 cm

12

36 cm²
54 cm²
24 cm²

Challenge

Use cm-squared paper.
Design and make an open box like those above that
will hold exactly:
a 30 Multilink cubes
b 36 Multilink cubes.

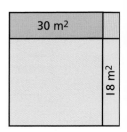

Can you solve problems involving numbers and quantities and explain methods and reasoning?

A Answer these.

1   42 × 10
2   56 × 100
3   423 × 10
4   15 × 100
5   640 ÷ 10

6   5200 ÷ 100
7   6300 ÷ 10
8   8000 ÷ 100
9   4320 ÷ 10

B Find each amount.

10   20% of £18
11   25% of £24
12   40% of £30
13   75% of £60

14   15% of £200
15   60% of £30
16   90% of £400
17   2% of £1200

C Find how many times larger each number is.

18   4500 than 45
19   62 000 than 62

20   590 than 59
21   260 than 2·6

D Find how many you will receive if you change £1200 into:

22   £100 notes
23   £50 notes
24   £10 notes
25   £5 notes

26   50p coins
27   10p coins
28   1p coins.

E Answer these.

29   0·6 × 10
30   6 ÷ 10

31   24 × ● = 24 000
32   48 000 ÷ ■ = 48
33   8 ÷ ◖ = 0·8

F Write as a fraction in its lowest terms.

34   40%
35   75%

36   15%
37   35%

38   34%
39   48%

G Find each amount without using a calculator. Estimate first.

40   20% of 245 g
41   10% of 132 l
42   12$\frac{1}{2}$% of £244

43   33$\frac{1}{3}$% of 723 miles
44   22% of 5000 km
45   110% of 550 ml

H Find each amount. Use a calculator. Estimate first.

46   16% of 350 km
47   49% of £2100
48   95% of 2500 cl
49   54% of £2600

50   155% of 2600 g
51   66$\frac{2}{3}$% of £939

I To the nearest penny work out the cost of each item in the sale.

52   £6·98   20% off

53   £116·40   15% off

54   £361   25% off

55   £9999   10% off

56   £39·50   33$\frac{1}{3}$% off

57   £32·65   20% off

58   £43·50   15% off

59   £1264   10% off

Challenge   ⊟ ⊠

Chloe is writing all the numbers from 3000 to 4000. How many 3s will she write?

Can you multiply and divide decimals mentally by 10 or 100 and integers by 1000 and explain the effect?

109

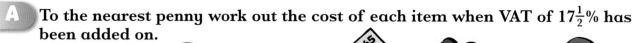

A

To the nearest penny work out the cost of each item when VAT of $17\frac{1}{2}$% has been added on.

1 **£6·80 + VAT**

2  **£4·56 + VAT**

3  **£22·65 + VAT**

4 **£54·26 + VAT**

5  **£116·45 + VAT**

B

Spark's have reduced their prices on all items by 20% for the sale. Find each original cost.

SPARKS

£46·40 £560 £137·20 £324 SALE

6 television
7 washing machine
8 video recorder
9 lamp

C

Sam buys his stock from the Shopkeeper's Catalogue. He adds 35% to the catalogue prices as profit. Find each price in his shop.

Shopkeeper's Catalogue			
Football	£9·80	Hockey stick	£17·60
Exercise bike	£196·40	Skis	£123·40
Football boots	£24·80	Walk machine	£228·20
Tracksuit	£26·80	Trampoline	£333·60

10 a hockey stick
11 a walk machine
12 skis
13 a trampoline
14 an exercise bike
15 a tracksuit
16 football boots
17 a football

If Sam reduces the cost of each item in his shop by 25% for a sale, find the profit or loss he will make to the nearest penny when he sells:

18 a football
19 skis
20 a trampoline
21 a walk machine
22 an exercise bike
23 a hockey stick.

Challenge

In the sale, Sam wants to sell some items as close as possible to the price he paid for them but without making a loss. By what percentage, to the nearest whole number, should he reduce his prices on these items? How much profit will he make on each? For example, a bicycle: catalogue price £124 selling price £124 + 35% = £167·40 reduce price by 25% = £125·55 profit = £125·55 − £124 = £1·55

    a telescope: catalogue price £210
    b javelin: catalogue price £155
    c scooter: catalogue price £85·80
    d weights: catalogue price £164

Can you find simple percentages of whole number quantities?

A Solve these problems.

50 pens cost £40. Find the cost of:

1 10 pens
2 200 pens
3 1 pen
4 1000 pens.

100 tins of soup have a mass of 42·4 kg. Find the mass of:

5 10 tins
6 1 tin
7 500 tins
8 1000 tins.

A rocket has completed 15% of its journey after travelling 24 000 km. Find how far it will have travelled when it has completed:

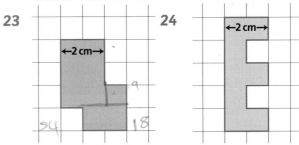

9 25% of its journey
10 90% of its journey
11 61% of its journey
12 100% of its journey.

B Find the perimeter and area of the new rectangle if you increase the sides of this rectangle in the ratio of:

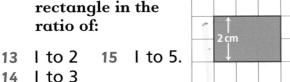

13 1 to 2   15 1 to 5.
14 1 to 3

C Find the area of the new square if you increase the sides of this square in the ratio of:

16 1 to 2   20 1 to 10
17 1 to 4   21 1 to 20
18 1 to 5   22 1 to 100.
19 1 to 8

D Find the area of each shape if the sides are increased in the ratio of 1 to 3.

23

24

E Find the perimeter of this shape if the sides are increased in the ratio of:

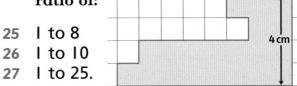

25 1 to 8
26 1 to 10
27 1 to 25.

Challenge

a Predict the perimeter and area of the new shape if you increase the sides of this shape in a ratio of 1 to 4.
b On cm-squared paper draw the shape that has sides 4 times longer than this shape. Check your predictions.

3 cm

You need:
- a partner
- 2 sets of 30 counters
- 2 copies of the game card

Game card			

Both write 12 of the numbers from the number machine in the different sections of your game card.

0·9 0·5
168 157
188 165
0·8 8·58
57 0·3
30·234
15·664 40

204 50
70 100
52 31·137
2·72 0·9
14·67
49 138

Agree on how to choose the winner of the game.

Take turns to place a counter by one of the questions below. Answer the question. If the answer is on your card or your partner's card, cover it with another counter.

Change the rules and play again with the new rules.

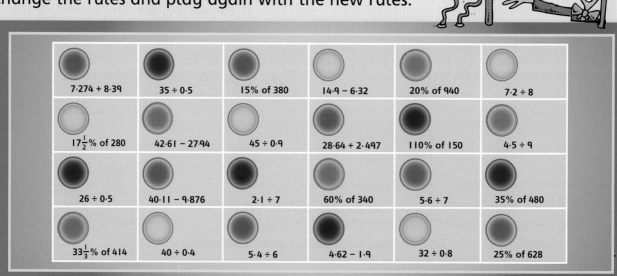

7·274 + 8·39	35 ÷ 0·5	15% of 380	14·9 − 6·32	20% of 940	7·2 ÷ 8
$17\frac{1}{2}$% of 280	42·61 − 27·94	45 ÷ 0·9	28·64 + 2·497	110% of 150	4·5 ÷ 9
26 ÷ 0·5	40·11 − 9·876	2·1 ÷ 7	60% of 340	5·6 ÷ 7	35% of 480
$33\frac{1}{3}$% of 414	40 ÷ 0·4	5·4 ÷ 6	4·62 − 1·9	32 ÷ 0·8	25% of 628

A Answer these. Use a method of short multiplication.

1	273 × 6	4	659 × 3	7	8·2 × 6
2	425 × 7	5	726 × 8	8	3·9 × 7
3	824 × 5	6	4·7 × 5	9	8·6 × 9

B Answer these. Show your working.

10	35 × 23	12	64 × 26
11	45 × 32	13	29 × 43

C Answer these. Use a method of short division.

14	363 ÷ 5	16	628 ÷ 9
15	943 ÷ 4	17	362 ÷ 7

D The octopus and starfish are learning to use proper numbers. Although they can add, subtract, multiply and divide they can only use 8s and 5s. So far they have worked out that 1 is the same as 8 + 8 − 5 − 5 − 5. Help them to understand other numbers by using only 8s and 5s.

Write how they can show the value of:

18	5 + 5 − 8

- 18 2
- 19 3
- 20 4
- 21 5
- 22 6
- 23 8
- 24 10
- 25 15
- 26 20
- 27 100.

E Find each number.

- 28 8 + 8 + 8 + 8 − (5 × 5)
- 29 (8 × 8) − (5 × 5)
- 30 (8 × 8) − (5 + 5)
- 31 88 − (55 + 5)
- 32 8 + 88 − 55
- 33 85 − (58 + 5)

Challenge

The spider and the kangaroo can count only in 8s and 3s. Work out how they can show numbers starting from 1. If you reach 100, have a rest!

Can you choose and use appropriate number operations to solve problems?

113

A Answer these.

1 463 × 36
2 285 × 49
3 364 × 37
4 742 × 16
5 835 × 26

B Answer these. Use a method of short multiplication.

6 6·36 × 8
7 7·45 × 7
8 9·26 × 5
9 4·93 × 6
10 3·07 × 8
11 11·59 × 5

C Answer these. Use a method of short division.

12 68·4 ÷ 3
13 29·5 ÷ 5
14 63·2 ÷ 8
15 53·1 ÷ 9
16 60·9 ÷ 7
17 43·8 ÷ 6

D Find the value of each.

18 2^2
19 3^2
20 2^3
21 3^3
22 5^2
23 6^2
24 5^3
25 4^4
26 2^5
27 6^3
28 9^2
29 10^3

E Express each number as the product of its prime factors.

30 $2 × 3 × 3 × 3 = 2 × 3^3$

30 54
31 60
32 24
33 16
34 36
35 40
36 42
37 75
38 72
39 100
40 120
41 600

Challenge

a Copy this square onto cm-squared paper.

b Find the area of the square.

c Divide the square in half and colour one of the halves. Find the coloured area.

$\frac{1}{4}$ $\frac{1}{2}$ $\frac{1}{16}$ $\frac{1}{8}$ $\frac{1}{32}$

d Divide the remaining section in half and colour one of the halves.
Each of these sections is $\frac{1}{4}$ of the square. Find the area of $\frac{1}{4}$ of the square.

e Find the total area now coloured.

f Continue dividing and colouring the square in this way until you have coloured a section that is $\frac{1}{128}$ of the square.

g Copy this table and continue it as far as you can.

Division	Fraction of whole square to colour	Total area of whole square coloured
1	$\frac{1}{2}$	32 cm^2
2	$\frac{1}{4}$	32 cm^2 + 16 cm^2 = 48 cm^2
3	$\frac{1}{8}$	56 cm^2
4	$\frac{1}{16}$	
5		
6		

Can you carry out long multiplication of a 3-digit by a 2-digit integer?

Use a calculator to help you.

A The builders with red hats can lay 360 bricks in a day. The builders with the blue hats can lay 240 bricks in a day. The builders with yellow hats can lay 200 bricks in a day. Find how many bricks all the builders can lay in:

1 1 day   3 20 days   5 300 days
2 6 days   4 100 days   6 330 days.

B Cooper's deliver fridges. They have 15 lorries. Each lorry makes 1 delivery every day. Five of the lorries can carry 24 fridges. Four of the lorries can carry 16 fridges. Three of the lorries can carry 12 fridges. Three more lorries can carry 6 fridges.
Cooper's deliver fridges 5 days each week.
They work 44 weeks each year.

Answer these questions.

7 How many fridges can be delivered in a year by the 4 lorries that can carry 16 fridges?

8 How many fridges can be delivered by all the Cooper's lorries in 4 weeks?

9 If 2 of the lorries that can carry 24 fridges are off the road for a week and the lorries that carry 16 fridges can only carry 10, how many fridges altogether are delivered during the week?

10 If all the lorries carry a full load how many fridges can Cooper's deliver in a year?

Challenge

There are 115 200 bricks in this block of flats. How many days would it take to lay the bricks if these builders from section A were building?
a builders in red hats
b builders in blue hats
c all the builders

Can you identify and use appropriate operations to solve problems involving number and quantities and explain methods and reasoning?

115

A Find each amount.

1 £4

1 $\frac{1}{6}$ of £24

2 $\frac{1}{3}$ of £90

3 $\frac{1}{5}$ of £55

4 $\frac{1}{10}$ of £140

5 $\frac{1}{4}$ of £84

6 $\frac{1}{6}$ of £54

7 $\frac{1}{8}$ of £88

Jules spends $\frac{5}{6}$ of £624 on a ring.

Walter spends $\frac{5}{8}$ of £872 on a boat.

Ivy spends $\frac{3}{5}$ of £945 on garden plants.

Rocky spends $\frac{2}{3}$ of £738 on climbing gear.

Frank spends $\frac{9}{10}$ of £570 on a stamp collection.

Ollie spends $\frac{3}{4}$ of £644 on a tree.

B Estimate the amount of money each person will spend. Find which person has spent:

8 the most money
9 the least money.

C Find the cost of each item.

10 the ring
11 the boat
12 the garden plants
13 the climbing gear
14 the tree
15 the stamp collection

Challenge

Use a calculator.
Work out the value of each letter.
Arrange the letters in the order of their values, largest first.
Below each letter write the letter that comes before it in the alphabet.
What is the hidden message?

$\frac{7}{9}$ of P = 266

$\frac{4}{17}$ of T = 60

$\frac{11}{12}$ of G = 451

$\frac{5}{11}$ of L = 45

$\frac{18}{19}$ of V = 198

$\frac{12}{13}$ of U = 312

$\frac{4}{11}$ of O = 140

$\frac{7}{13}$ of B = 252

$\frac{7}{13}$ of D = 84

$\frac{9}{14}$ of M = 27

$\frac{16}{19}$ of Y = 368

$\frac{7}{12}$ of R = 133

$\frac{5}{13}$ of Z = 15

$\frac{5}{9}$ of J = 95

$\frac{11}{17}$ of F = 198

Can you use a fraction as an 'operator' to find fractions of numbers or quantities?

A — Reduce to the simplest form.

1. $\frac{10}{12}$
2. $\frac{16}{18}$
3. $\frac{21}{27}$
4. $\frac{64}{80}$

5. $\frac{6}{40}$
6. $\frac{35}{80}$
7. $\frac{20}{36}$
8. $\frac{35}{63}$

9. $\frac{24}{90}$
10. $\frac{125}{200}$
11. $\frac{42}{66}$
12. $\frac{24}{64}$

13. $\frac{15}{80}$
14. $\frac{36}{100}$

1 $\frac{5}{6}$

B — Write the complement to 1 of each fraction. Give your answer as a fraction in its simplest form.

15. $\frac{128}{192}$
16. $\frac{24}{96}$

17. $\frac{66}{99}$
18. $\frac{108}{144}$

19. $\frac{35}{100}$
20. $\frac{144}{240}$

15 $\frac{1}{3}$

C — Solve these problems.

RANGERS

In a football crowd of 23 328 people, 2916 were Rangers supporters and the rest supported Rovers. Write as a fraction in its simplest terms the fraction of the crowd that supported:

21. Rangers
22. Rovers.

23. In a survey of 6250 people, 3750 voted to allow a by-pass around their town. The rest voted against the by-pass. Write as a fraction in its simplest terms the fraction of people who voted against the by-pass.

24. A town has a population of 18 600. There are 4650 children. Write as a fraction in its simplest terms the fraction of the population who are children.

D — $B = \frac{2}{3}$ of A. Find the value of B if A is:

25. 6
26. 12
27. 30
28. 66.

E — $\frac{3}{5}$ of X = Y. Find the value of X if Y is:

29. 27
30. 36
31. 60
32. 120.

Challenge ⊟ ☒

Play with a partner. Use a calculator and 2 sets of 12 counters. Take turns to choose one of the fractions from the yellow box. Reduce the fraction to its simplest form. If your answer is on the grid, cover it with a counter. The first player with three counters in a line wins.

$\frac{162}{216}$	$\frac{189}{252}$	$\frac{128}{192}$	$\frac{192}{480}$	$\frac{216}{252}$	$\frac{96}{240}$	$\frac{256}{320}$
$\frac{72}{180}$	$\frac{125}{200}$	$\frac{175}{250}$	$\frac{160}{256}$	$\frac{288}{336}$	$\frac{99}{363}$	$\frac{150}{180}$
$\frac{75}{90}$	$\frac{275}{330}$	$\frac{144}{168}$	$\frac{72}{96}$	$\frac{140}{252}$	$\frac{240}{360}$	$\frac{108}{126}$
$\frac{80}{144}$	$\frac{288}{432}$	$\frac{196}{280}$	$\frac{175}{210}$	$\frac{180}{288}$	$\frac{54}{198}$	$\frac{56}{80}$

$\frac{3}{4}$	$\frac{2}{5}$	$\frac{5}{8}$	$\frac{5}{6}$
$\frac{2}{3}$	$\frac{2}{5}$	$\frac{3}{11}$	$\frac{6}{7}$
$\frac{7}{10}$	$\frac{5}{6}$	$\frac{5}{9}$	$\frac{5}{8}$
$\frac{6}{7}$	$\frac{4}{5}$	$\frac{3}{4}$	$\frac{2}{3}$

Can you reduce a fraction to its simplest form by cancelling common factors?

117

A Use a bag of 4 red counters, 4 yellow counters, 4 black counters and 4 blue counters. Without looking into the bag, take out 12 counters.

Write as a fraction in its simplest terms the proportion of your counters that are

1 red
2 yellow

3 black
4 blue.

In its simplest terms find the ratio of:

5 black counters to blue counters
6 red counters to yellow counters
7 yellow counters to black counters

B Solve these problems.

8 In a crate of 144 apples, 3 out of every 8 apples are bad. How many bad apples are there in the crate?

9 If the ratio of Jamie's weight to his dad's weight is 5 to 12 and Jamie weighs 30 kg, how heavy is his dad?

10 Find the ratio of these two lengths.

_____

_____

11 A class of 30 children are divided into 2 equal groups. The first group is then divided into 2 more groups in the ratio of 2 to 3. The second group is divided into 2 more groups in the ratio of 2 to 1. There are now 4 groups. How many children are in each group?

12 Flour can be released from these containers 1 kg at a time. What is the least amount of flour that needs to be released so that the ratio of the mass of flour in the yellow container to the mass of flour in the blue container is 5 to 3?

Challenge   ▢ ✕

Choose the first 100 words on any page in your reading book. Work out in its simplest terms:
a the ratio of words containing 1 vowel to the words containing 2 vowels
b the ratio of 4-letter words to 5-letter words
c the ratio of words beginning with a vowel to words beginning with a consonant
d the ratio of 6-letter words to 2-letter words.

You need:
- a partner
- a dice
- 2 sets of 6 counters
- 2 score sheets

Each player places a counter on the START square.
Take turns to roll the dice and count around the money trail.
Work out the amount of money you collect from each section you land on.
Keep a total of the money you collect on your score sheet.
As soon as you have enough money, buy any item you can afford in the window display. Subtract the cost from your money total. Place a counter by the item to show it is sold. The first to buy 5 items is the winner.

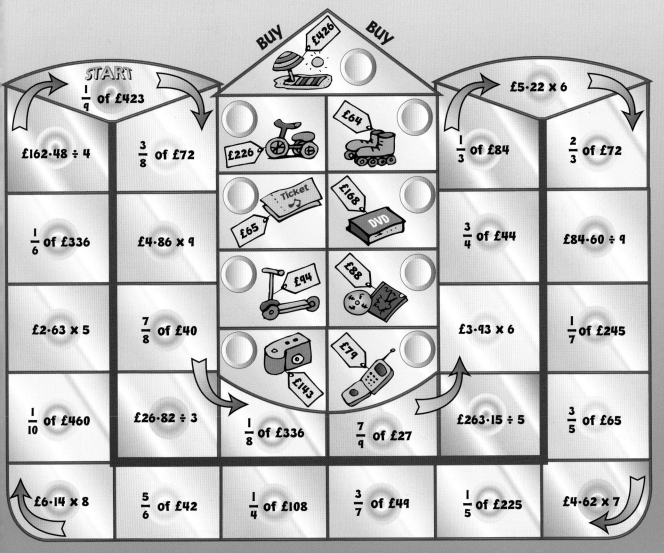

BUY £426 BUY

START
$\frac{1}{9}$ of £423

£5·22 × 6

£162·48 ÷ 4 | $\frac{3}{8}$ of £72 | £226 | £64 | $\frac{1}{3}$ of £84 | $\frac{2}{3}$ of £72

$\frac{1}{6}$ of £336 | £4·86 × 9 | Ticket £65 | £168 DVD | $\frac{3}{4}$ of £44 | £84·60 ÷ 9

£2·63 × 5 | $\frac{7}{8}$ of £40 | £94 | £88 | £3·93 × 6 | $\frac{1}{7}$ of £245

$\frac{1}{10}$ of £460 | £26·82 ÷ 3 | £143 | £79 | £263·15 ÷ 5 | $\frac{3}{5}$ of £65

$\frac{1}{8}$ of £336 | $\frac{7}{9}$ of £27

£6·14 × 8 | $\frac{5}{6}$ of £42 | $\frac{1}{4}$ of £108 | $\frac{3}{7}$ of £49 | $\frac{1}{5}$ of £225 | £4·62 × 7

A Measure these angles to the nearest 1°. Use a protractor.

1 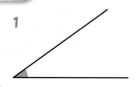 2   3 4   5

B As accurately as you can, draw each angle.

6	55°	9	46°	11	111°
7	75°	10	33°	12	24°
8	150°				

C Measure each angle to the nearest 1°.

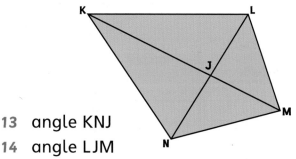

13 angle KNJ
14 angle LJM
15 angle KLJ   17 angle KJL
16 angle NMJ   18 angle KNM

D In each diagram estimate the size of the angle XYZ. Measure with a protractor to check your estimate.

19 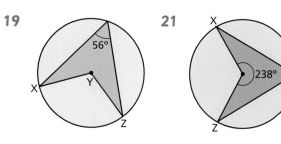   21

20 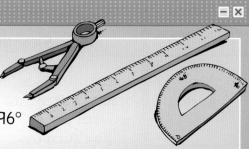   22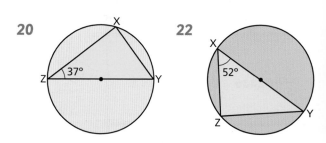

Challenge

Use a pair of compasses, a ruler and a protractor.
Draw each shape.
a a triangle with angles of 42°, 68° and 70°
b a quadrilateral with angles of 54°, 85°, 125° and 96°
c an isosceles triangle with one angle of 102°
d a triangle with all its vertices on the circumference of a circle, the diameter of the circle as one of its sides and one of its angles measuring 36°

120

Can you use a protractor to measure acute and obtuse angles to the nearest degree?

A Use a pack of playing cards. Answer these questions.

1 How many different results can you get with the colour of the card if you turn over the top card of the pack?

> 1 2: red or black

2 How many different results can you get if you turn over the top 2 cards of the pack? These are 2 of the possibilities:

3 Copy and complete this table to show the different possible results for turning over the top 3 cards.

1st card	2nd card	3rd card
R	B	R
R	R	B

Find how many different results you can get when you turn over the top:

4 3 cards
5 4 cards
6 5 cards
7 10 cards.

B Find how many different results you can get with the suits of the cards when you turn over the top:

8 1 card
9 2 cards
10 3 cards
11 4 cards
12 5 cards
13 10 cards.

Challenge ▢☒

Table

	P	W	D	L	F	A	GD	Pts
Barlow	10	10	0	0	32	10	22	30
Dibton	10	9	1	0	28	12	16	28
Holt	11	7	4	0	22	11	11	25
Farlow	11	6	5	0	18	10	8	23
Byfield	10	5	3	2	22	16	6	18
Pegham	11	4	1	6	15	14	1	13
Pitsea	10	4	0	6	17	17	0	12
Hope	11	3	2	6	12	14	⁻2	11
Matton	10	3	0	7	6	16	⁻10	9
Keld	11	2	2	7	11	28	⁻17	8
Coombe	10	1	0	9	8	23	⁻15	3
Aston	11	0	0	11	4	24	⁻20	0

Results

Keld (0) 1	Barlow (1) 3
James 56	Jackson 25
	Mills 58 og
	Carlow 89
Pegham (0) 1	Matton (0) 0
Birch 66 pen	
Coombe (0) 0	Pitsea (1) 2
	Romney 45
	Frith 67
Byfield (1) 1	Aston (0) 0
Plowden 34	
Farlow (1) 2	Dibton (0) 2
Ravino 30	Jenkins 67 pen
Saya 56	Hobley 88 og
Hope (0) 0	Holt (0) 0

a How many goals were scored in 45 minutes or less?

b How many own goals were scored?

c How many penalties were scored?

d How many goals were scored altogether in the matches?

e If there are 3 points for a win and 1 point for a draw, rewrite the league table showing how it would have looked before these matches were played.

Can you solve a problem by sorting data and interpreting tables and charts?

121

A Plot each set of points on a grid with four quadrants. Join up the points in order with straight lines. Name the shape you have drawn.

1 (⁻1,5) (⁻3,2) (⁻1, ⁻4) (1,2) (⁻1,5)

2 (⁻2,3) (2,3) (4,1) (2,⁻2) (⁻2,⁻2) (⁻4,1) (⁻2,3)

3 (⁻3,4) (2,4) (5,⁻4) (⁻5,⁻4) (⁻3,4)

4 (5,2) (⁻2,⁻5) (⁻5,⁻2) (2,5) (5,2)

B On the plan of the golf course 1 cm represents 100 m. For each hole find:

5 the coordinates of the tee and the flag

6 the length of each hole to the nearest 10 m.

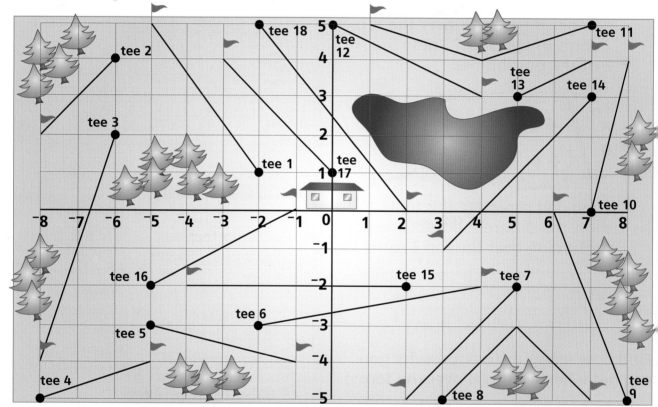

Challenge

Use cm-squared paper. On your paper mark out a rectangle 16 cm by 8 cm. Your rectangle represents a field measuring 1600 m by 800 m. You have drawn the field to a scale of 1 cm to 100 m. Design a golf course with a pond, trees and 9 golf holes so that:

a hole 3 is the shortest hole

b hole 5 is 260 m

c holes 6 and 8 are the same length

d hole 9 is 420 m.

Can you read and plot coordinates in all 4 quadrants?

A Answer these:

1 4.26×10 4 $238.4 \div 100$
2 $3.45 \div 10$ 5 4.94×100
3 28.4×100 6 6.165×100

B Write in descending order.

7 4·23, 4·4, 44·23, 42, 42·3
8 16·29, 16·92, 1·692, 6·92, 9·62
9 21·3, 211·3, 121·3, 12·23, 32·1
10 8·307, 3·807, 3·87, 8·37, 83·07

C Write in its lowest terms.

11 $\frac{12}{20}$ 13 $\frac{24}{80}$ 15 $\frac{30}{55}$

12 $\frac{25}{60}$ 14 $\frac{48}{72}$ 16 $\frac{24}{36}$

D Find the answer. Use a calculator.

17 45% of £64   20 15% of £4500
18 18% of £200   21 $12\frac{1}{2}$% of £360
19 32% of £644   22 $17\frac{1}{2}$% of £566

E Answer these.

23 4293×4 28 $171 \div 9$
24 3685×7 29 $448 \div 8$
25 1798×6 30 $413 \div 7$
26 3275×9 31 $356 \div 4$
27 8126×4 32 $492 \div 6$

F The shape inside the rectangle is an isosceles triangle. Without using a protractor work out each angle.

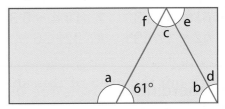

33 angle a   35 angle c   37 angle e
34 angle b   36 angle d   38 angle f

G Find the range, mode, median and mean number of each set of test scores.

39 Mark 9, 4, 5, 5, 7, 6, 7, 6, 5
40 Anna 1, 7, 2, 2, 6, 7, 3, 0, 8
41 Salma 9, 3, 8, 4, 6, 7, 3, 7, 7
42 Ali 9, 5, 4, 10, 8, 7, 4, 1, 6

H Write a formula for the nth term in each sequence.

43 5, 7, 9, 11, 13 …
44 6, 9, 12, 15, 18 …
45 1, 3, 5, 7, 9 …
46 2, 6, 10, 14, 18 …

I Solve these problems.

47 Books are reduced by 15% in a sale. How much do you save when you buy 3 books for £3·20, £9·60 and £11·40?
48 On a sheet of stickers there are 6 columns and 8 rows. If each sticker costs 22p, how much is the sheet of stickers worth?

A Answer these.

1 6·385 + 2·149
2 14·78 + 3·948
3 24·618 + 19·8
4 11·42 + 17·695
5 13·264 − 7·518
6 21·23 − 6·895
7 14·4 − 6·389
8 324·36 − 19·758

B Work out the area of this shape.

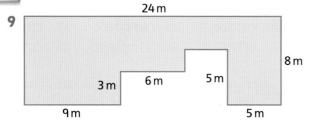

9

24 m
8 m
3 m 6 m 5 m
9 m 5 m

C This square has been split into rectangles.

15 cm²

24 cm²

10 Work out the lengths of the sides of each rectangle.

11 Find the area of the square.

D Answer these.

12 9 ÷ 10
13 0·8 × 10
14 16 × ⭐ = 16 000
15 32 000 ÷ ⬤ = 32
16 6 ÷ ⬤ = 0·6

E Find each amount.

17 30% of 125 kg
18 10% of 233 ml
19 12½% of £320
20 66⅔% of 213 km
21 120% of 325 cl

F If the sides of this rectangle are increased in the ratio of 1 to 4 find:

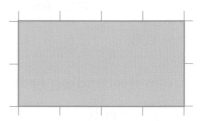

22 the perimeter of the rectangle
23 the area of the rectangle.

G Answer these.

24 246 × 28
25 329 × 37
26 476 × 17
27 279 × 46
28 348 × 32
29 463 × 52
30 4·28 × 7
31 6·59 × 8
32 49·6 ÷ 8
33 73·5 ÷ 7

H Express as a product of its prime factors.

34 40
35 64
36 54
37 75
38 200
39 320

I Find each amount.

40 $\frac{3}{5}$ of £65
41 $\frac{2}{3}$ of £48
42 $\frac{7}{9}$ of £81
43 $\frac{19}{100}$ of £500
44 $\frac{6}{7}$ of £133

J Reduce to their simplest form.

45 $\frac{25}{80}$
46 $\frac{36}{60}$
47 $\frac{25}{200}$
48 $\frac{24}{72}$
49 $\frac{12}{100}$
50 $\frac{64}{200}$

K Measure each angle in the yellow shape to the nearest 1°.

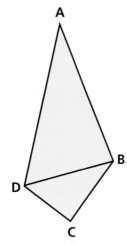

A
B
D
C

51 angle ABC
52 angle DBA
53 angle DBC
54 angle ADB
55 angle BCD

Lucy Unlockett, the world's leading safe expert, has designed a new padlock. The code combination uses a letter, followed by three numbers, and then another letter.

If all the letters of the alphabet can be used and the digits 0 to 9, investigate how many different settings are possible for the padlock.

Here are five examples:

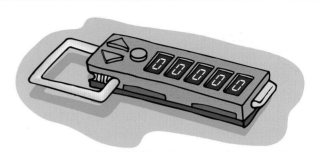

A 3 4 6 A   G 0 0 5 E   C 1 2 3 K   R 9 2 7 X   P 0 5 5 E

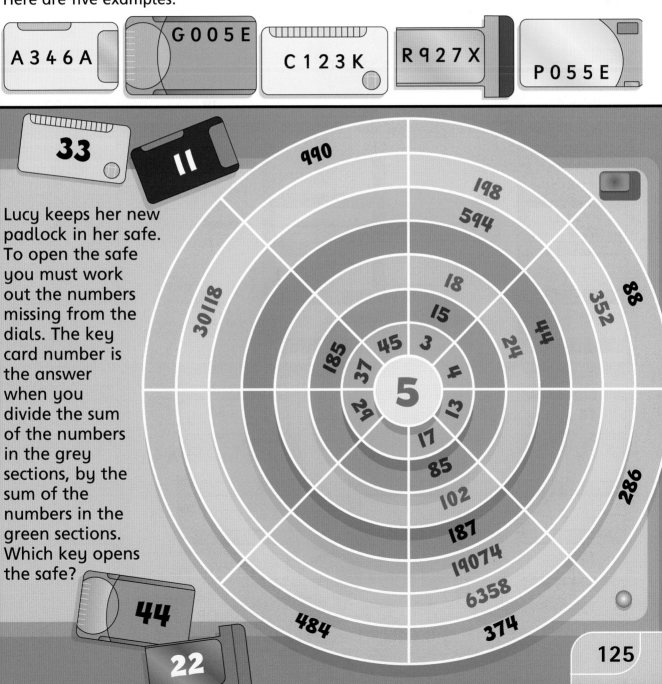

Lucy keeps her new padlock in her safe. To open the safe you must work out the numbers missing from the dials. The key card number is the answer when you divide the sum of the numbers in the grey sections, by the sum of the numbers in the green sections. Which key opens the safe?

33   11   44   22

990   198   594   18   15   3   4   13   17   85   102   187   19074   6358   374   484   30118   185   37   45   29   5   24   44   352   88   286

This board is from a maths game. All the rules and the equipment have been lost.

Make up a set of rules for the game. Find or make any equipment you need.

Try your game with a partner and make any improvements you can.

8
6
4
2

8
6
4
2

21
16
24
12

18
15
30
8

20
28
6
24

42
21
25
18

30
56
24
20

36
45
16
50

48
12
27
32

START

24-hour clock – measures time starting from 0 to 24 hours, e.g. 05:30 is 5:30 a.m. and 17:30 is 5:30 p.m.

a.m. – short for 'ante meridiem' meaning 'before noon', used to show times between 12 midnight and 12 noon

acute angle – an angle less than 90°

analogue clock – a clock that has hands to show the passing of time

angle – an amount of turn, flat shapes have angles at the corners

anti-clockwise – turns in the opposite direction to the hands on a clock

approximate answer – a rough answer or estimate near to the exact answer

area – the amount of surface a shape covers, measured in square units such as cm^2, m^2

array – a regular arrangement of objects in rows and columns

ascending sequence – a set of numbers arranged in order from smallest to largest

axis (axes) – graphs have two axes, one horizontal and one vertical

bar chart – a graph that uses bars or columns to show information

capacity – the amount a container holds, measured in l and ml

Carroll diagram – used for sorting things into groups, e.g. red and not red, cubes and not cubes

century – a set of one hundred, e.g. 100 years

clockwise – turns in the same direction as hands on a clock

column – a vertical line of objects or numbers one above the other

compass points – a compass is used to find directions; north (N), south (S), east (E) and west (W) are the four main points on a compass

complement – the remaining part of a set, e.g. the complement to 100 of 60 is 40

compound shape – a shape made up of different rectangles

consecutive – things that come one after another in a regular order, e.g. 11, 13, 15 are consecutive odd numbers

coordinates – pairs of numbers that show the position of a point on a graph, read across first (horizontal coordinate), then up (vertical coordinate)

data – information about something in words, numbers or pictures

decimal place – the number of digits to the right of the decimal point

denominator – the bottom number of a fraction

descending sequence – a set of numbers arranged in order from largest to smallest

diagonal – a straight line that joins two corners of a shape

digit – each figure in a number is called a digit, e.g. 416 is a 3-digit number

digital clock – a clock that has only numbers to show the time

divisible – a number is divisible by another number if it can be divided exactly with no remainder, e.g. 49 is divisible by 7

edge – the edge is where two faces of a solid shape meet, e.g. a cube has 12 straight edges

equivalent fractions – fractions with the same value, e.g. $\frac{6}{10} = \frac{3}{5}$

estimate – using information you have to guess an answer without measuring or doing a difficult calculation

even number – any whole number that can be divided exactly by 2, e.g. 2, 4, 6, 8, 10, …

face – a side of a solid shape, e.g. a cube has 6 square faces

factor – a whole number that divides exactly into another number, e.g. 1, 2, 3, 4, 6 and 12 are factors of 12

formula – a short way to write a rule

frequency – how often something happens

horizontal – a level or flat line parallel to the horizon or ground, a line parallel to the bottom edge when represented on paper

imperial – measuring system with units such as inches, feet, yards, pints, gallons, pounds and ounces

improper fraction – a fraction with the numerator larger than the denominator

integer – a positive or negative whole number

inverse – the opposite, addition and subtraction are inverse operations

irregular polygon – a 2-D shape with sides or angles that are not equal

line graph – a graph that shows information as points joined up by lines, line graphs often show how things change over time

line symmetry – a shape has line symmetry if it can be folded so one half covers the other exactly

Glossary

lowest terms – a fraction has been reduced to its lowest terms when the numerator and denominator have no more common factors

mass – the amount of matter in an object, measured in g or kg (sometimes people use weight to mean mass)

mean – an average (add all the quantities and divide by the number of quantities)

median – an average (the middle value when numbers are put in order)

metric – measuring system based on tens, hundreds and thousands with units such as mm, cm, m, km, g, kg, ml, cl, l

mid-point – halfway between two points

mixed number – a number containing a whole and a fraction part, e.g. $2\frac{1}{4}$

mode – an average (the quantity or number that occurs most often)

multiple – a number that is exactly divisible by another, e.g. numbers in the times table, 5, 10, 15, 20, 25, 30 are all multiples of 5

negative numbers – numbers less than zero

net – a 2-D shape that can be folded up to make a 3-D shape

numerator – the top number of a fraction

obtuse angle – an angle between 90° and 180°

odd number – any whole number that cannot be divided exactly by 2, e.g. 1, 3, 5, 7, 9, 11, ...

origin – the point on a coordinate grid where the axes cross, (0,0)

p.m. – short for 'post meridiem' meaning 'after noon', used to show times between 12 noon and 12 midnight

parallel – lines that are the same distance apart along their whole length are parallel

partition – to break numbers down into, e.g. units, tens, hundreds and thousands

percentage – the proportion written as a fraction with a denominator of 100, 54% (54 per cent) means 54 out of every 100

perimeter – the distance around the outside of a shape

perpendicular – lines are perpendicular if they meet at right angles (90°)

pictogram – a graph that uses pictures to show information

pie chart – a graph that shows information as a circle, different-sized slices show different quantities

polygon – a 2-D shape with straight sides

positive numbers – numbers greater than zero

predict – to say what you think will happen

prime factor – a factor of another number that is a prime number, e.g. 1, 2 and 5 are prime factors of 20, but 4, 10 and 20 are not

prime number – a number with only two factors, 1 and itself

probability – the chance or likelihood of an event occurring

product – the answer when two or more numbers are multiplied together, e.g. the product of 40 and 8 is 320

proportion – e.g. a drink contains 100 ml of juice and 500 ml of water, the proportion of juice is $\frac{1}{6}$, the proportion of water is $\frac{5}{6}$

quadrant – the axes of a coordinate grid form four sections called quadrants

quadrilateral – a polygon with four sides

quotient – the answer from a division calculation, e.g. $27 \div 3 = 9$, the quotient is 9

range – the difference between the greatest and least values in a set of data

ratio – e.g. a drink contains 100 ml of juice and 500 ml of water, the ratio of juice to water is 1:5 (1 to 5)

reflection – the mirror image of a shape

reflex angle – an angle greater than 180°

regular polygon – a 2-D shape with all sides and angles the same

remainder – the number left over after division, e.g. $27 \div 4 = 6$ r 3, the remainder is 3

right angle – a quarter turn measured as an angle of 90°

rotation – moving a shape by turning it

round up/down – writing a number as an approximate, e.g. 5792 rounded to the nearest thousand is 6000

row – a horizontal line of objects or numbers side by side

sequence – a set of numbers written in an order following a rule, e.g. 1, 4, 7, 10 is a sequence adding 3 each time

square number – the result of multiplying a number by itself, e.g. $9 = 3 \times 3$

translation – moving a shape by sliding it to a different position up, down or across without turning it

Venn diagram – used for sorting things into sets

vertex (vertices) – the corner of a shape, where sides or straight edges meet

vertical – a line that points straight up at right angles to a horizontal line, a line parallel to the sides when represented on paper